MA
T

AN INTRODUCTION TO

TYPOGRAPHY

TYPO
GRAPHY

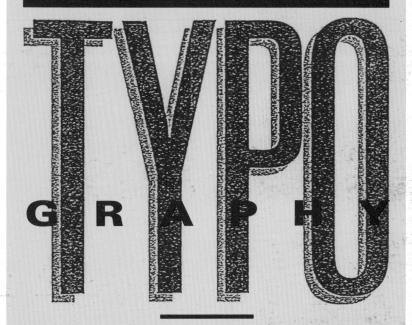

AN INTRODUCTION TO
TYPOGRAPHY

TYPOGRAPHY

TERRY JEAVONS
MICHAEL BEAUMONT

THE
APPLE
PRESS

A QUINTET BOOK

Published by The Apple Press
6 Blundell Street, London N7 9BH

ISBN 1-85076-203-1

This book was designed and produced by
Quintet Publishing Limited
6 Blundell Street, London N7 9BH

Creative Director: Peter Bridgewater
Designer: Terry Jeavons
Project Editor: Caroline Beattie
Contributing Editor: Charles Foster
Contributors: Terry Jeavons and Frances Marr
Picture Researcher: Liz Eddison
Artwork: Danny McBride and
Jenny Millington

Typeset in Great Britain by
Central Southern Typesetters, Eastbourne
Manufactured in Hong Kong by
Regent Publishing Services Limited
Printed in Hong Kong by
Leefung-Asco Printers Limited

CONTENTS

MARRIED Families

BELOW: Creating a corporate identity for a client gives the typographic designer an opportunity to design a namestyle that is unique. The logotype for the Collier Campbell company was specially drawn by the typographer. In addition, the 'look' of stationery items is enhanced by the careful use of type size and layout.

ABOVE: Two beautifully simple, yet inventive ways of using type to emphasise the meaning of words. By flipping the second 'R' in 'MARRIED' and joining the two letters together the designer has wittily conveyed the marriage union. Similarly, the graphic produced by the i, l and i in the word 'families' immediately communicates.

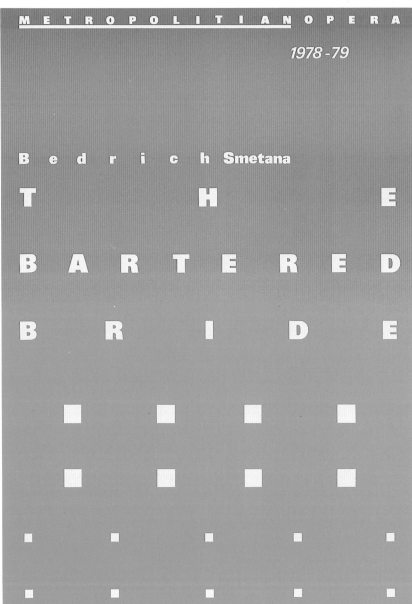

METROPOLITIAN OPERA

1978-79

Bedrich Smetana

THE BARTERED BRIDE

ABOVE: This striking poster for the US Metropolitan Opera's production of Smetana's The Bartered Bride, illustrates how simply by designing with type and colour, results in a distinctive and eye-catching piece of publicity.

Introduction

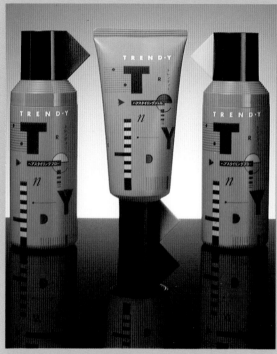

ABOVE: The highly fashion conscious market for these beauty products was the inspiration for using avant garde typography and rich bright colours to give these packs powerful customer appeal.

Typography, like all disciplines in design, is colourful and exciting when it is handled with professionalism and creativity. Think of all the printed advertisements you can remember, or the calendar you couldn't bear to throw away. Then you can see the potential power that letters, numbers and images have when they are put together carefully and produced well.

The technology of type and typesetting has changed dramatically since the days when letters were produced in hot metal and sat in wooden trays. Typesetting is now a digitized process and coupled with the personal computer boom, has become far more accessible to far more people. Designers can now control, mould and reshape type without moving away from their desks.

It should be said that typography and design skills cannot be picked up overnight. There are basic principles that have been developed, for good reason, over the centuries. These need to be understood – before they can be broken. On the other hand, as in any creative process, intuition plays a great part. Perhaps the first rule then should be 'If it looks right, it is right.'

Typography should never be seen apart from other areas of visual and graphic design. They are dependent on each other for their impact and should be created and developed together.

This book provides a basic understanding of the design, construction and use of type. There is some terminology to learn, but it should not be too over-whelming. Equipped with some basic techniques and tools, you can have the confidence to go on and become a first class typographer.

MICHAEL BEAUMONT

The Creative
Opportunities

1 The Creative Opportunities

What exactly is type? Obviously it is a means of communication, but there is a deeper answer than that. Typographic characters are a series of abstract shapes used in various combinations to represent the sounds with which we communicate. As they are abstract in nature they also have other meanings and associations. For example, the letter O could be a face, a stone, a ball or the sun. The letter S could be a snake.

In fact all typographic characters have visual associations, some originating from the pictorial symbols used in Egyptian hieroglyphics. It is because they have abstract and pictorial possibilities that the letters of the alphabet have become the fundamental units of visual communication.

Where do we find type? Everywhere. Books, magazines, brochures, leaflets and stationery, packaging, posters and billboards. And further: sign posts, shop fronts, van livery, logotypes, television and cinema titles, and decoration for clothing and jewellery. Also there are the fine arts: 3D sculptures, ceramic decorations, stained glass, cut glass, tombstones, hot air balloons, commemorative plaques, graffiti and much more besides. We are surrounded by typographic images. The more meaningful and attractive we can make our typographic imagery the better our visual awareness will become, in just the same way that architecture and furniture affect everyday attitudes and behaviour.

ABOVE: A rather decorative monogram caved into the timber frame of a West of England building. Note how the bar of the H has been replaced by a small floral motif.

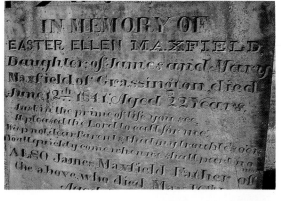

ABOVE: Tombstone carving has for many centuries provided some of the most decorative and exquisite examples of calligraphic stone masonry. It is a craft that dates back to the times of the Romans and their inscriptions.

RIGHT: Type does not have to be perfectly executed to be attractive. The charm of this example lies very much in the general ambiance of its nautical location and associative bric-a-brac. This is very much a case of unintentional decoration.

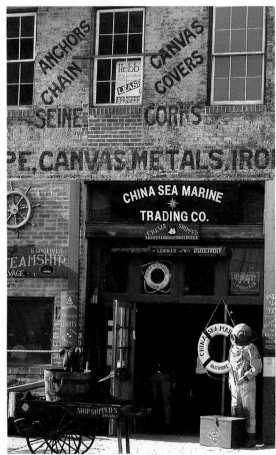

ABOVE: Pageantry provides opportunities for flamboyant colour and decoration. This is very much the case for the annual City of London's Lord Mayor's Show. The elegance of this embroidery from one of those costumes is a fine example of the decorative splendour of the event.

RIGHT: Until relatively recently, road signs, company name plates and street numbers were cast in metal. Most have now been replaced by various combinations of neon, plastic and screen printing but there are still examples in existence such as this name plate for the Hambros Bank Building in the City of London.

LEFT: The American Dream. Typical 1950s illustration and neon display. The family car with its mandatory two children, one of each, of course! This style of graphics has had a recent revival as a new generation of young designers look back to former styles with respect and affection.

LEFT: A stained glass window from Spring Mountain, California. We normally associate stained glass with churches but this is not always the case. This subtly coloured example is used to promote Chardonnay wine.

LEFT: An interesting example: at first sight this Canadian name plate has the appearance of a metal casting but on closer inspection we can see that the oval mould is a concrete cast with hand-lettered typography.

LEFT: City night life is dominated very much by its sky line. The neon image sings out and this script lettering for the promotion of Schlitz lager is typical of this form of advertising.

LEFT: The Victorians were great decorators. Unfortunately not many examples of their work still exist due to the bulldozers. However, some Victorian public buildings have survived where decorative tiles can still be seen. This particular example forms part of the décor at the Victoria & Albert Museum in London.

David Quay is one of
Britain's leading
typographic designers. He
has designed many
typefaces particularly for
the Letraset library. His
designs include: Agincourt,
Arta, Bordeaux, Quay,
Santa Fe, Titus and Vegas.

These examples of his
personal stationery are
interesting. On the one
hand they represent the
style of today with its
variable type size running
round an arc, on the other
hand the overall feeling for
space and angles owes
much to the Bauhaus
movement of the twenties.

A knowledge of design
history is very much part of
a designer's vocabulary and
reference library, and its
importance should not be
underestimated.

Type comes in many shapes
and forms. John Greener is
a photographer and
consequently felt that his
stationery should illustrate
that point. This clever use
of letter form projection
and shadow clearly
describes his business. The
designer for this work was
David Quay.

John Elliott Cellars Ltd, 11 Dover Street,
Mayfair, London. Telephone: 01 493 5135
Wholesalers of Fine Wines & Champagne
Buvons, amis, et buvons à plein verre.
Enivrons-nous de ce nectar divin!
Après les Belles, sur la terre,
Rien n'est aimable que le vin;
Cette liqueur est de tout âge:
Buvons-en! Nargue du sage
Qui, le verre en main,
Le haussant soudain,
Craint, se ménage,
Et dit : holà!
Trop cela!
Holà!
La!
La!
La!
Car
Panard
A pour refrain:
Tout plein!
Plein!
Plein!
Plein!
Fêtons,
Célébrons
Sa mémoire;
Et, pour sa gloire,
Rions, chantons, aimons, buvons.

LEFT:Being able to understand this advertisement for a wine wholesaler is not important. The wine glass silhouette immediately tells us that the product is wine. Even if we can't understand the meaning of the copy we all know enough to recognise the language as French so we must therefore assume the product to be French. A clever and effective piece of advertising. The copy was adapted from an 1818 French drinking song.

BELOW: The Napoli '99 Foundation was established to create an awareness of the city's environmental and social problems. To promote the foundation, international designers were commissioned to produce posters as an integral part of a travelling exhibition.

This ink splattered example from Pentagram was designers Mervyn Kurlansky and Herman Leslie's answer to the portrayal of Napoli's pollution problems.

What is the function of type? Type is not always simply to be read. Attracting attention, enhancing and decorating, and telling a story may be just as important.

Readability is the biggest single necessity for typography that provides information. Designers must always keep this as their top priority. Copy which is meant to be read but is hard to read – no matter how clever or fashionable the layout might appear – is badly designed.

Readability need not mean dullness. On the contrary, the more attractive, the more exciting, the more creative the feel for tone, colour and space, the more readable that design will become. Although body copy usually occupies the largest area of space it often requires the least amount of the designer's time.

Type is also used to attract attention, often in a headline where the design compliments the message. It may do this by being brash, crude or vulgar – or elegant and flowing. Its integration with colour – especially in packaging – may be significant. Whatever its function, the use of type should be integrated with the other design elements and developed simultaneously.

The successful use of type to enhance and decorate requires skill, usually to ensure that it maintains its readability. Calligraphy may be appropriate for an inscription or a commemorative plaque. Packaging often requires enhanced or decorative type, and gives designers opportunities to develop their own typefaces. However type is used, its legibility remains of paramount importance.

Type may also be used to tell a story, one of the most exciting, fulfilling areas of typographic design.

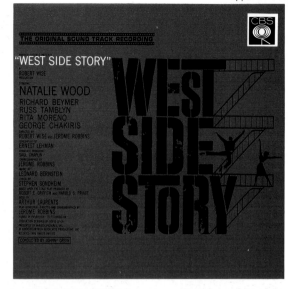

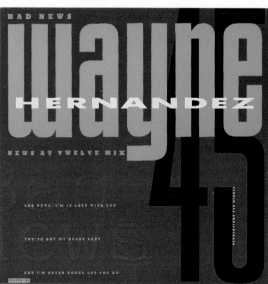

ABOVE: Of course display type does not always tell a story or graphically illustrate the point being made. The type on this example is used solely as decoration in a fairly contemporary manner.

ABOVE TOP: The Musical 'West Side Story' was set within the tenement blocks of New York's West Side ghetto. The bold condensed face from the publicity material clearly conveyed the congestion of the rising tenement blocks cleverly integrated with the maze of metal fire escapes.

RIGHT: Decorative packaging does not necessarily have to be complex. This example for Joseph Parfum de Jour consists of just three lines of type set in a small rectangular block. The italic J is just enough to give the design that extra touch of class appropriate to its projected market.

18

ABOVE: By contrast the design for the Quatro can, still based upon the rectangle, approaches the decorative objective in an entirely different manner. The four strong colours represent the four flavours of the drink as they enclose the hand drawn simplistic Q.

ABOVE: Sometimes a pack design requires a feel for history. This can be achieved either by taking the style of an earlier period and recreating it on the modern pack, or by recycling the actual graphics used for the original pack into the new design.

This design for Sunlight soap falls into the second category: it is a product that had been on the British market for over a hundred years, and the current design has reverted to one based upon the original layout. It uses similar but cleaner, more modern colours, together with an updated modification of the typography.

LEFT: Whilst the above example has a feel for the past, this 1906 cocoa tin shows the differences between the two periods. The colour was less intense and the construction of the letterforms lacked some of the traditional values of balance and proportion.

LEFT: Originally called Sumner's Typhoo Tea after its creator; the foliage-adorned grey carton of this tea pack was launched in Birmingham, England, in 1905. Promoted as bringing relief for indigestion, it was originally purported to be the 'tea that doctors recommend'. However, medical claims on packaging were banned in the 1940s. By the 1970s much of the foliage design had disappeared to reveal the now familiar red pack. An illustration of teapot and cups has recently been added.

BELOW: Tobacco is best preserved when kept in airtight containers, and so tins were used extensively by tobacco manufacturers at the turn of the nineteenth century. This pack for Edgeworth pipe tobacco dates from around 1890 and its design has remained virtually unchanged to this day. The dominance of the hand-drawn outline typefaces were very common for that period.

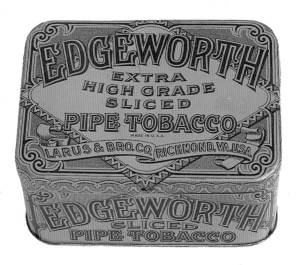

Typahgrrphy

ABOVE: Herb Lubalin designed this logo for a graphic arts quarterly. Within this particular issue, discussing the merits of good and bad typography, he offered the opinion that 'the best typography never gets noticed', hence the spelling in this example.

BELOW: Herb Lubalin's most famous design. A definitive piece of graphics such as this can not be reproduced too often and should serve as an inspirational source for all designers. Ironically the design never appeared as originally intended. The original commission was for a never-to-be-published magazine. Lubalin himself felt that the suggestion of the foetus in the womb was one of his finest typographic designs. The work is now in the permanent collection of the Museum on Modern Art in New York.

The knack is to illustrate words or messages in such a manner that someone without any comprehension of the language can fully understand the visual message. The great American graphic designer, Herb Lubalin, was a past master of this particular style of graphic communication with such historic designs as 'Mother & Child', 'Families' and 'Marriage'. Even in work with large areas of text he always looked for ways in which the written word could be embellished or illustrated to describe the point being made more graphically.

This ability to create visual associations is very important when designing symbols and logotypes. The purpose of a logotype is to provide a graphic device which can be recognized as the symbol of a company or association's work. Therefore, if the logotype can simultaneously tell a story to clarify the business or activity the more effective that image is. This may not always be possible, particularly in larger multinational companies with a broad range of products and services. One logo that works effectively was designed for electrical company 'Plessey' where the name is written in the form of an electrical current; another was the logo designed for the footwear division of the 'Dunlop' company. This consisted of the type being extended into a foot shape. It is interesting to note that logos that have been with us for many decades are rarely seen today in their original form. They have all been subtly modified and updated over the years, as can be seen, for example, in those for Coca-Cola, Ford and Esso.

With an understanding of the meaning and function of typography, other ways of enhancement of an image become possible. 'If it looks right, it is right'.

Such freedom provides an infinite variety of media.

20

MORE TO COME

MORE TO COME

MORE TO COME

ON PBS
PUBLIC
BROADCASTING
SERVICE

ABOVE: An animated sequence for an on-air television spot for the American Public Broadcasting Service designed by Lubalin. One of his favourite ploys was to manipulate the letter 'O'. In this instance the O is animated whilst the viewer is waiting for the final message to arrive.

M O THER
CHILD

THE NEW YORK COMMITTEE OF YOUNG AUDIENCES 400 WEST END AVENUE, NEW YORK, N.Y. 10024 212 874-5503

LEFT: Another example of Lubalin's fascination for the graphic use of the letter 'O'. A rather comlex, fun logo for a committee that introduced young audiences to theatre and opera productions. Note how he was prepared to use the scalpel to trim and join letterforms in order to achieve perfect justification of the column. A very common ploy of Lubalin and one that can often be used to achieve a better balance within a design concept.

22

RIGHT: One of the most successful graphic logos explaining the business of the company. The electrical pulse lines cleverly follow the contours of the word Plessey, the multi-national electrical company.

ABOVE: We do not always have to use all of the typographic character to promote an idea or image; sometimes the incompleteness of a character can add to its impact. This is a case in point. A logo for the Victoria and Albert Museum which has successfully severed part of the capital A without reducing readability. This omission actually helps counterbalance the strong stress of the V.

LEFT: These four examples illustrate the natural development of the Ford logo over the years. Whilst the basic signature has remained constant, its weight has strengthened over the years.

RIGHT: D is the Design Council's new magazine for students. Pentagram partner David Hillman, who was responsible for the design of the magazine, prepared a booklet and poster to promote the new publication prior to its launch. The imagery for the poster is both dynamic and educational. Educational because the four quarters of the D illustrate the numerous possibilities from the simplest of ideas.

RIGHT: Railway tracks combined with a lower case 'r' make a strong and simple brand identity for the Railex Railroad Line stationery, a product of the Simpson Paper Company.

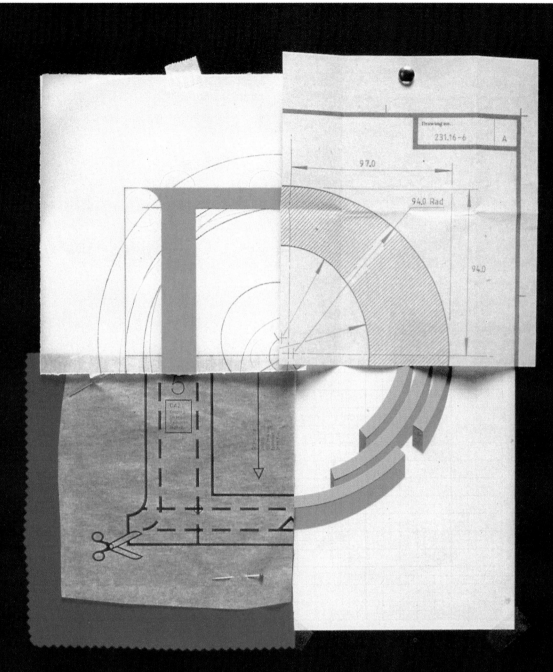

Whatever you do, take a look at **D**

The new magazine for
student designers.
First issue
Friday 13th October.
For more information write to
Morven MacKillop,
The Design Council,
28 Haymarket,
London SW1Y 4SU
or telephone
01-839 8000

ABOVE: Fun with letters.
There are a few occasions
when instant readability is
not a pre-requisite and this
is one such occasion. Bob
Gross, chairman of the
Geers Gross advertising
agency, commissioned
Pentagram to design an
invitation card for his
daughter's 21st birthday
party.

RIGHT: Colour can be used to both decorate and create the typographic form. The elements of the Bifur alphabet, drawn by Cassandre in 1929, were borrowed by Pentagram as the basis for this logotype identifying 'Cannon Babysafe's Avent' range of feeding utensils.

RIGHT: When designing logotypes always try to add a second dimension to the typography or design. If that can be accomplished a greater impact and meaning will be achieved to promote and associate the company name with its product. This is a case in point. A logo was required for the music publishing company, Faber Music. The starting point in the design was obviously the letter 'F' but in musical terms a lowercase italic 'f' is for *forte* (loud), and a double italic 'f' means *fortissimo* (very loud). Thus by using the double f italic ligature the logo identified both the company, Faber, and the product, music publishing.

BELOW: A witty use of the proof correction mark for 'transpose' (see page 76), in this identity for Gary Gray, a copywriter.

BELOW: This logo for Hilton Typographers, a typesetting company, cleverly uses a variety of serif styles to communicate Hilton's involvement in the type business.

26

ABOVE: 'No one has decreed
that type must always be
flat, typeset and printed
black on white.' To prove
this point Mervyn
Kurlanksy made a
collection of items from the
Pentagram studio to form a
three dimensional alphabet
affectionately known as
Kurlansky Kaps.

No one has decreed that type must always be flat, typeset and printed black on white. Admittedly a hand-written novel would be difficult, if not impossible, to read but amounts of calligraphic body copy have been successfully used for advertising and promotional purposes. Whilst it has to be accepted that for large areas of body copy black on white is best for optimum readability, there are beautiful examples of text for brochures and leaflets printed in sepias, greys and subtle shades of blue without any loss of legibility.

Although there are numerous typefaces available with in-built decorative and creative features, the type itself can be manipulated, distorted or decorated to produce an even greater level of creativity. Always have an open mind. Can the product be treated in a different manner? If it is for a garden fertiliser can the company name be grown in a flower bed to illustrate its efficiency? Can the promotional headline for a steel works be constructed out of its product? Could a wool company have its message hand-knitted? These and countless other possibilities are open to the creative mind: always look deeper for the creative opportunities that lie beneath the surface of most graphic problems. Most of us at some time in our lives have inadvertently experimented with three dimensional imagery – say, drawing a name in the sand on a beach.

Sometimes three-dimensional embellishment can be just simple substitution of an object for a letterform. One of the earliest examples of this was designed for CBS radio by the American designer, Louis Dorfsman, in the early 1950s. To illustrate the point that radio was about listening Dorfsman graphically used large display lettering for the word 'HEARING' and replaced the three characters E, A, R with a photograph of an actual ear. This graphic symbol had far more power and impact than the words alone could ever have achieved.

There are many examples where the surface of the basic letterform has been enhanced, decorated or textured. The airbrush is particularly useful for such work. An airbrush artist can make type sparkle with the luminosity of highly polished chrome or take on the appearance of wood or fabric.

Areas of body copy can also be used to tell a story. A computer can handle practically all design requirements. Body copy can be set in all manner of shapes limited only by the imagination of the designer; copy within circles, bottles and figures or in wavy lines, is easily produced.

The wonderful thing about modern design is that if imagination can create the ideas, modern technology (budgets permitting) can provide most of the solutions. There are very few technical limitations any more. Such flexibility provides wonderful opportunities for the graphic designer's creativity.

27

ABOVE: There is nothing new in seeing the potential of three dimensional objects to form alphabetic possibilities. This Victorian handbill for Calvert's Mechanic's Almanack dates back to 1874. Even some of the same objects appear as in the Kurlansky example opposite.

Movable type – Johannes Gutenberg

The true Effigies of Iohn Guttemberg Delineated from the Original Painting at Mentz in Germanie.

Johannes Gutenberg (1398–1468) can be regarded as the most important historical figure in graphic design and in particular, printing. A goldsmith by trade, his invention of printing from individual pieces of movable cast type in Western Europe revolutionized the printing industry. Prior to this invention manuscripts were handwritten and laboriously copied by scribes. Gutenberg's invention allowed multiple copies of books to be produced relatively inexpensively. Those books consisted of engraved illustrative pages and minimal text which were inked and transferred onto paper by the means of a screw press.

It took Gutenberg ten or more years of trial and error and great expense before – around 1440 in Mainz,

Germany – his invention saw the light of day. Such was the impact of his invention that by the end of that century more than a thousand printing shops had produced some 10 to 20 million books. The impact of his movable type invention and letterpress printing can be measured by the fact that it lasted well into the twentieth century and has only relatively recently been superseded in by lithographic printing.

His training as a goldsmith provided him with a sound working knowledge of how to cast metal objects. This prompted him to consider how he could cut punches and stamp letters and images on hot metal. Gutenberg knew that to be successful, his new method of printing had to be indistinguishable from the highly finished writings of the scribes. To achieve this he had to cast several versions of the various characters and ligatures to simulate the style of the scripts he had chosen to copy. Eventually he had a font of over 300 characters (the average for a modern computer font is around 125 characters).

Gutenberg had to cut a separate punch in steel for every character, which he then struck in a softer metal to make a matrix. The matrix was then fitted into a mould, and to avoid having to make a separate mould for every character width he had to devise a mould of variable width. The adjustable mould became the foundation of his invention.

He also had to find a metal which would melt easily and flow evenly into the matrix and when cool expand fractionally to produce a perfect fit within the matrix, but would still be hard enough to withstand the constant pressure of printing onto paper or skin without wearing out too quickly. The alloy he used has been the basis for all metal setting since those times. It is made of lead with a small percentage of antimony for strengthening hairlines with tin for toughness and to make the lead melt more easily.

His ink, consisting of a mixture of linseed oil and pigments used by painters in oils, had a depth of black and a permanence which has never been improved upon to this day.

It is not clear how much work Gutenberg carried out before his first great work, his 42-line Bible; it is the earliest book printed in the Western world to have survived. It consisted of 1286 pages – the largest size printed on paper was 409 × 209mm – and issued in two volumes. It has been estimated that Gutenberg printed up to 200 copies. The type was 'Textura', a condensed, upright and angular style characterized by the almost total absence of curves.

N ec sum adeo informis, nuper me in littore uidi,
C um placidum uentis staret mare. non ego Daphnin
I udice te metuam, si nunquam fallat imago.
O tantum libeat mecum tibi sordida rura,
A tq; humileis habitare casas, & figere ceruos,
O edorumq; gregem uiridi compellere hib:sco.
M ecum una in syluis imitabere Pana canendo.
P an primus calamos cera coniungere plures
I nstituit, Pan curat oues, ouiumq; magistros.
N ec te poeniteat calamo triuisse labellum.
H aec eadem ut sciret, quid non faciebat, Amyntas?
E st mihi disparibus septem compacta cicutis
F istula, Damoetas dono mihi quam dedit olim,
E t dixit moriens, te nunc habet ista secundum.
D ixi: Damoetas, inuidit stultus Amyntas.
P raeterea duo nec tuta mihi ualle reperti
C apreoli, sparsis etiam nunc pellibus albo,
B ina die siccant ouis ubera, quos tibi seruo.
I am pridem à me illos abducere Thestylis orat.
E t faciet. quoniam sordent tibi munera nostra.
H uc ades o formose puer. tibi lilia plenis
E ce ferunt nymphae calathis, tibi candida Nais
P allentes uiolas, et summa papauera carpens,
N arcissum, et florem iungit bene olentis anethi,
T um casia, atq; alijs intexens suauibus herbis,
M ollia luteola pingit uaccinia caltha.
I pse ego cana legam tenera lanugine mala,
C astaneasq; nuces, mea quas Amaryllis amabat.
A ddam cerea pruna, et honos erit huic quoq; pomo.
E t uos o lauri carpam. & te proxima myrte,

a iiii

The advent of movable type meant that consistency in typefaces was not possible and in 1466 Conrad Sweynheim and Arnold Pannartz cut the first Roman typeface. It was not entirely satisfactory – it had too many Gothic overtones – and it was left to a Frenchman, Nicholas Jenson, to produce the first successful roman typeface in 1470. The other influential typeface designer of the period was the Italian, Francesco Griffo, whose cursive Humanistic script, Cancellaresca Corsiva, gave us the first italic typeface. Those two are credited with making the roman style dominant in most of Europe except Germany, Scandinavia, and the Slavic countries where the Gothic styles were popular for many centuries.

LEFT: Gutenberg looking at Faust's first proof printed with moveable type.

LEFT AND BELOW: An example of the Italian, Francesco Griffo's first italic typeface taken from a page designed by Aldus Manutius's for the Juvenal and Persius opera (1501). This was one of the first books to use Griffo's new italic face. Note the capital Roman letters at the beginning of each line. The enlargement shows the rather crude form of those early letterform punches but that takes nothing away from the achievement of those revolutionary pioneers.

29

LEFT: A section from the Gutenberg 42-line Bible. Notice the very strong vertical stress of the Textura letterform together with the minimal line spacing causing legibility difficulties. Such problems will still occur with modern condensed typefaces if the line feed is not increased.

2

The Development
of Type Design

2 The Development of Type Design

We tend to think of graphic design as a 20th-century phenomenon but nothing could be further from the truth. Visual communication predates the written word as a means of conveying information as the discovery of prehistoric images carved on fragments of bone and paintings on the walls of caves shows.

In the Roman Empire, in the quest for progress and learning, typography first developed into the standard Roman alphabet as we know it today. This was then transmitted to the conquered peoples of Europe and subsequently spread through the teaching of Christianity. Other letterforms developed at the same time in other civilizations.

The first Roman letter forms were all what we now call capitals, but by the early fourth century AD a cursive variation, introduced by the Greeks and known as the uncial, began to emerge. Designed for everyday use, these more rounded letterforms with short ascenders and descenders lent themselves to quicker writing. This led in due course to the development of distinct upper and lower case forms for each letter of the alphabet.

The Romans set standards for the construction of typefaces which are still used today. Features such as serifs, backwards stress and variation in letter weight all owe much to the angle of the pens and chisels used by the Romans for inscription.

By the middle ages all of the elements of modern writing were in evidence. Through the influence of the church this was a tremendously rich period in the development of art that has left a wonderful legacy of illuminated letterforms and scripts. In the early period the most popular styles were Roman square capitals, uncials and half uncials (the half uncial evolved from the early Roman cursive and square capitals and not the uncial as the name implies).

BELOW: A fragment from the pediment of the Forum in Rome. From this example we can clearly see how the angle of the chisel has affected the overall stress of the characters and shape of their serifs.

RIGHT: A much earlier example of graphics than the Roman carving below. This Egyptian granite relief dates back to the XXth Dynasty. This hieroglyphic can be seen in the Louvre, Paris and is from the Sarcophagus of Rameses III.

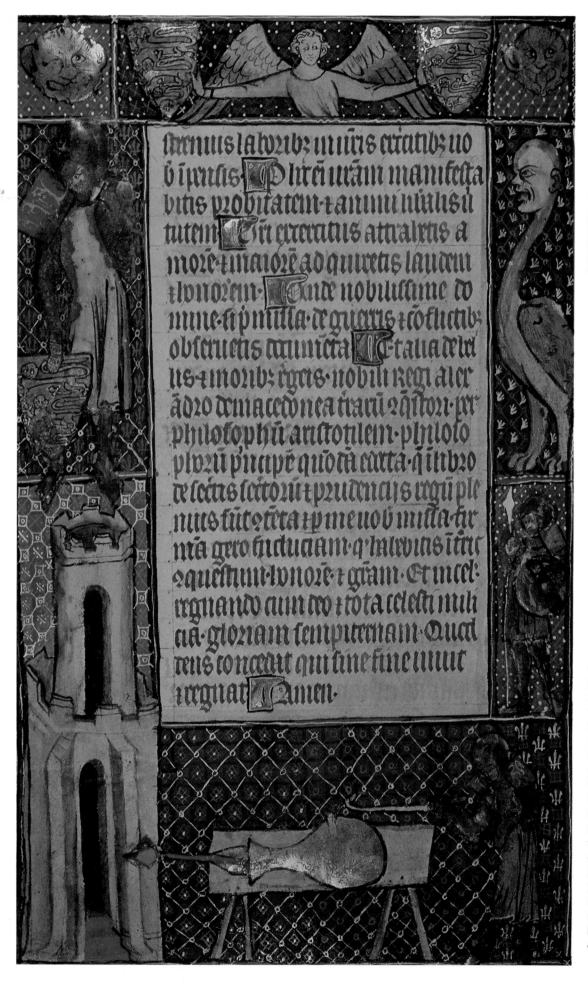

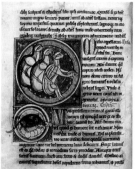

ABOVE: Three cats from a 13th-century bestiary. A layout that in many ways is not very different from much of today's graphics with its dropped initials and body copy — calligraphic writing in this instance — running around the two rectangles.

LEFT: An earlier example is this cannon (*De Nobilitatibus*) from Walter de Millemete. It dates back to 1326. Note the slightly more condensed letterform consistent with the earlier period.

OPPOSITE PAGE: The Christian monks of the Middle Ages have left a most remarkable legacy of inscriptions, writings and illuminations. They are full of colour and give a wonderful insight into aspects of life in those times. This piece from the Soane Museum in London represents the procession of St Gregory against the plague in Rome and dates from around AD 1500. Notice the more open style of the type producing a more readable text than the slightly earlier 'Textura' of Gutenberg's 42-line bible. The main feature of nearly all of the early religious works from the monasteries were their beautiful illumination of capitals.

By the late middle ages letterforms has become narrow and angular with short ascenders and descenders. Historically known as Textura, they are more commonly referred to today as Gothic or Old English letterforms. The advantage of the Textura letter was its economy of space but because of its strong vertical stress and ornate style it was difficult to read.

Throughout the fourteenth and into the next century a non-religious group of scholars known as 'Humanists' immersed themselves in the study of the Greek and Roman cultures. Their study of the open handwriting of the Romans and the Carolingian scripts created a style which became the model for our present day lower case letters.

The mid-fifteenth century marked the birth of graphic design as we know it today. The reason was Johann Gutenberg's invention of printing from individual pieces of movable cast type.

The new limitations of the printing presses, paper and ink, meant that type designers had to rethink their designs. The fine strokes of the pen on vellum or parchment associated with the Roman forms were no longer possible. This led to type designs with little contrast between thick and thin strokes and rather heavy serifs. Today we refer to these designs as Old Style. Examples of such typefaces are the original Garamond and Cloister Old Style.

After this breakthrough, technological progress was steadily made over the next two or three centuries. Presses became more efficient and the quality of the paper and ink improved. Type designs developed; towards the end of the seventeenth century there was a movement towards typefaces showing greater

contrast between thick and thin strokes, with more delicate serifs. These typefaces are now called Transitional designs.

The last major Old Style face is considered to be Caslon, a face still, in various redrawn forms, very popular. Designed by the Englishman William Caslon in the earlier part of the eighteenth century, it dominated both the English and American printing industry throughout that century.

Transitional is a convenient term to link the Old Style and Modern typefaces. The most well known Transitional face – and like Caslon still popular – was designed by another Englishman, John Baskerville. The clean open forms of Baskverville with greater contrast between thick and thin than Old Style, and its clear readability, demonstrates why it remains so popular.

During this period two French families also left their mark upon the graphic arts. They were the Fournier and Didot families. Pierre-Simon Fournier created the first point system Didot Firmin is credited with designing the first typeface we classify as Modern, with its extreme contrast between thick and thin and unbracketed hairline serifs. The introduction of these Modern typefaces explain the logic behind the term Transitional for faces like Baskerville which bridged the design gap between the Old and Modern styles.

A few years after Didot's design, the Italian, Giambattista Bodoni, designed the most famous of all Modern faces, which bears his name. Containing many of the same characteristics as the Didot face, Bodoni's design, due mainly to his fame as a printer, is still associated with present-day typeface design.

Just as Gutenberg's invention can be seen as the birth of modern graphic design, we can look to the nineteenth century as the time when graphics began to cover all forms of communication: brochures, periodicals, leaflets, advertising, posters etc. The Industrial Revolution in Europe and America brought about vigorous expansion with the advent of steam, electrical and oil power. The communications industry kept pace with new challenges also.

Major design developments in the first forty years of this century include the Art Nouveau, Art Deco, Futurism, Dadaism and the Bauhaus movement. Typographers who stood out during that period were Eric Gill, Stanley Morison and Jan Tchichold and Rudolf Koch. Later this century the modern technologies have totally liberated typeface design so that typeface classification has become almost superfluous as designers combine features from many of the previous styles in their quest for faces with new character.

One style that affected the period between the two world wars is generally referred to as Art Deco. Its influence was felt both sides of the Atlantic in all spheres of life including architecture, fashion and

RIGHT: The central panel of the title page with the first mark of Badius Asensuis Lucretius' *De Rerum Natura,* Paris 1514.

36

LEFT: Giambattista Bodoni (1740–1813) was born in Saluzzo, northern Italy, the son of a poor printer. As a young man he travelled to Rome and learned punch cutting. By the time he was twenty-eight he was asked to take charge of the Stamperia Reale, the official press of Ferdinand, Duke of Parma.

By the end of the eighteenth century graphic design was changing; Bodoni took a leading role in evolving new typefaces and page layout. In 1791 he redesigned the traditional Roman letter form to produce a more mathematical, geometric, and mechanical typeface. He reshaped the serifs by making them hairlines that formed sharp right angles with the upright strokes. There was no tapered flow of the serif into the upright stroke as in Old Style roman.

Known as Bodoni, the basic style is still popular today, so much so that many type manufacturers have adapted the original design and issued it in various weights, widths and italic forms.

Hic ille est Magnus, typica quo nullus in arte

Plures depromsit divitias, veneres.

LEFT: A sample of the original Bodoni text.

ottimamente fatte. Che però la grazia della scrittura forse più che in altro sta in certa disinvoltura di tratti franchi, risoluti, spediti, e nondimeno così nelle forme esatti, così degradati ne' pieni, *che non trova l'invidia ove gli emende.* Ma forse più sicuro

John Baskerville

ABOVE: John Baskerville
(1706–75) was an
innovator who broke all of
the prevailing rules of
design and printing at his
Birmingham press. He
designed, cast, and set
type, improved the printing
press, conceived and
commissioned new papers,
and designed and
published the books he
printed. In addition he was
also a master writer,
stonecutter and
manufacturer of japanned
ware. He is best known for
the still-popular typeface
that bears his name, a
transitional face that
bridged the gap between
the Old Style roman and
the Modern typefaces.

RIGHT: A specimen page
from the Quarto Virgil
published by John
Baskerville in 1754 with the
headings reduced to
letterforms symmetrically
arranged and letterspaced.
Economy and simplicity
were a feature of his
works.

PUBLII VIRGILII MARONIS BUCOLICA GEORGICA ET AENEIS

Ad optimorum Exemplarium fidem recensita.

TO THE PUBLIC.

JOHN BASKERVILLE proposes, by the advice and assistance of several learned men, to print, from the Cambridge edition corrected with all possible care, an elegant edition of Virgil. The work will be printed in quarto, on this writing royal paper, and with the letter annex'd. The price of the volume in sheets will be one guinea, no part of which will be required till the book is delivered. It will be put to press as soon as the number of Subscribers shall amount to five hundred whose names will be prefixt to the work. All persons who are inclined to encourage the undertaking, are desired to send their names to JOHN BASKERVILLE in Birmingham; who will give specimens of the work to all who are desirous of seeing them.

Subscriptions are also taken in, and specimens delivered by Messieurs R. and I. DODSLEY, Booksellers in Pall Mall, London. MDCCLIV.

graphic design. A less flowing style than Art Nouveau, it contained a greater feel for geometric and angular shape although it retained a freshness of colour.

During the period between the two world wars different countries made a distinct contribution. The Soviet Union's Constructivists, the Dutch magazine *De Stijl,* the major American magazines such as *Harper's Bazaar, Esquire, Vogue, Saturday Evening Post, Life* and *Time.* All made an impact.

Three particularly versatile contemporary typefaces were designed by the International Typeface Corporation. ITC Weidemann, ITC Goudy Sans and ITC Tiepolo all reflect in different ways the importance of historical tradition and form.

Kurt Weidemann designed a book face for just one publication, a Bible translation for the German Bible Society. ITC asked the Society to allow the face, originally called Biblica, to be made more widely available. It was renamed Weidemann.

Weidemann followed Old Style characteristics in his design. He reasoned that bracketed serifs helped to retain the baseline definition and that the relatively even strokes of the letterforms gave a more uniform colour resulting in less show-through on lightweight papers. He also reckoned that Old Style faces permitted more distinctive shapes for individual letters than was usual with many other serif faces. The face is certainly distinctive, and whilst it owes much to tradition, it is very much a typeface of today.

By complete contrast ITC Goudy Sans owes much to various styles. Unlike nearly any other sans serif it offers a very strong cursive style, the opposite of the oblique

THE  TIMES

LAST MONTH'S
AVERAGE DAILY SALE
433,000

No 63,560

FRIDAY NOVEMBER 24 1989

(30p)

39

Czech Army 'will defend

'By popular acclaim I am happy to carry on'

Thatcher says
she is read

roman style normally found in a sans serif face. This cursive feel is even more pronounced in its italic form especially in the capital characters G, Q and X.

The design was quite a departure for its designer, Frederic Goudy, whose sans faces were normally based upon the historical sans serif traditions, although having made that point this face is not without tradition. A strong connection between it and the Roman stone inscriptions is very apparent, right down to the slight flare for the serifs.

The design team AlphaOmega Typography Inc responsible for the creation of ITC Tiepolo described it as a 'sans serif with serifs'. Yet it could also be described as a calligraphic design; for example, look at the characters C, G and O.

What appears to be a rather carefree attitude to the various strokes which make up the characters is not in fact the case: they have actually been carefully developed within a modular framework. Contrary to how it might appear, Tiepolo is constructed with care and proportion. It is not something that just grew from a calligrapher's pen.

The letter shapes are based upon classic Roman proportions: counters are full, and the ascenders and descenders have been kept to sensible dimensions. To maintain tonal colour within text setting the capitals have been drawn slightly shorter than the ascenders. Round characters such as a, b and c have been rendered with almost slab sides to add distinction and provide a great deal of latitude for the intercharacter spacing possibilities.

The feature of all three of these designs lies very much in their versatility. They all contain family variation – eight for the Weidemann and Goudy, six for Tiepolo – and work well in a variety of settings; display, caption and text. In fact all three can be used successfully for large areas of text setting without loss of legibility, a feature not possessed by all typefaces.

The main point with all these faces is that whilst the designs are contemporary, they pay their respects to the importance of historical tradition and form.

MIKE POWELL

ABOVE: Examples of the 'Times' newspaper.

LEFT: Stanley Morison (1889–1967) was typographic advisor to the Monotype Corporation, one of the most famous typefounders, and the Cambridge University Press. He is best remembered as the man who supervised the design of a new typeface for a major twentieth-century newspaper and magazine.

Since the commission came The Times of London in 1931, he called this new typeface 'Times New Roman'. It first appeared in the October 3rd, 1932 London edition of the newspaper. The features of the new design were its short ascenders and descenders with sharp small serifs. This new typeface had the effect of radically changing overnight the typographic appearance of one of the world's leading newspapers, giving it greater legibility and clarity. Times New Roman has now become one of the world's most popular and widely used typefaces of the twentieth century.

LEFT: Times New Roman and Times New Roman italic.

The Times New Roman type, cut for the newspaper in 1931 is another true twentieth-century type face. It is available in the greatest range of sizes and weights, *always a factor in the continued success of a type design.*

ÉTUDE D'EXÉCUTION

LEFT: The late summer of 1917 marked the formation of the *De Stijl* art movement and journal in the Netherlands. The feature of the movement was its use of flat, geometric shapes and pure colour. One of the members who joined its leader, Théo van Doesburg, was the architect JP Oud who designed the facade for the Café de Unie, Rotterdam in 1925. This serves as a good illustration of how both typography and architecture were combined to develop the philosophy of the movement. The sans serif typeface also followed ideas developed by the Bauhaus ideology of that same period.

RIGHT: The experimental newspaper, *Lacerba,* was used by the Futurist movement to spread its ideas and philosophy. This example – *Words in Freedom* by Carrà – first appeared in a 1914 edition of the newspaper.

200   **LACERBA**

CORRENTI di rumori da Sud a Nord

CLOWN Altissimo Tour Eiffel

lingua di piccione bianco leccare leccare

leccare cervello

linguaggi poliritmici

nell'aria rinchiusa

CoZzO NoDi

CONVEGNO DI FORZE

amanti im pro vvisati

AVAMPOSTE EUROPA ARTISTICA

rumori
(acutitsimo alto
vertiginoso 300 m.)
vetri infranti
musica drammatica del Boulevard
Saint-Michel

sconposizioni e velocità
architetture (**fuggente sferico ellissoidale fluttuante**)

luci colorate

ARCOBALENI negli spessori dei corpi umani e dei pilastri

ISCRIZIONI (luuuuuuuuuungo fuggente balzante intrecciato bianco su fondo celeste)

CHATELET TOMBE-ISSOIRE

MONTROUGE

pace delle campagne primavera
ciuffi di neve Alpi Italia
attirare
respingere
colare colare colare
colarecolori lucelettrica

30 specchi

GARA di 318000 lettere
26 000 000 numeri
PRIMATO
lottare vincere
cancellare sopraffare
cristalli giocare tutto
ottoni maioliche conflitto
guerra commerciale per la

fosforescente
minuzioso
accanito
feroce
intransigente
acciaiato

VITTORIA

del PROPRIO PRODOTTO

nero
fumoso
zigzazante

bilanci *bilanci* *bilanci* *bilanci* BILANCI

titoli bancari porti porti porti docks
quotazioni di Borsa fumaiuoli maone

nella **NOOOTTE** dei **MAAARIii** che non
vedrò mai

inesplorato meneinfischio

SI NO N ooooo
NO SI FORS-NNATO
SI NO S iiiiii

18.000.000 di uomini in rissa
senza conoscersi
ricchezza del mio spirito

GRAVITARE di masse perpendicolari sul piano orizzontale del mio **TAVOLINO** di marmo

BIBITE R̶I̶B̶E̶L̶L̶I̶ contro volontà
SETE CEREBRALE LUSSO
8 odori di **41** femmine (occasionale cronametrato rastrellante) = **8** siluri = **LUS SILURI A** slittare slittare
slittare sul pensiero

DOMINANTE
della
mia
POVERTA

FORZA COMMERCIALE della personalità fisica di questi capolavori d'

A
LcovA

mercato notturno **FIERA** (meraviglioso giostrante illuminatissimo tintinnante)

EQUIVoCO della prudenza

Provinciale accidentalità inebriante

avvilimento visione (nostalgico sprezzante in-

OLDSTYLE SERIF (HUMANIST AND GARALDE):

The Old Style Serif contains bold and strong features with relatively uniform stroke widths. The serifs normally join the stem with a curve and the letters are generally of open proportion.

TRANSITIONAL:

The Transitional category bridges the gap between the Old Style and Modern Serif. Unlike the Old Style Serif there is greater variation between the vertical and horizontal stress of the characters and reduced bracketing upon the serifs.

MODERN SERIF (DIDONE):

A natural development from the transitional with a strong contrast between thick and thin strokes, and little or no bracketing. The weight stress of the Modern Serif in round letters is symmetrically located.

42

SQUARE SERIF (SLAB SERIF):

The main feature is the strong, heavy blocked design of the serif with little contrast between the vertical and horizontal strokes. The serifs join the main stem at a sharp angle or with a small radius.

SANS SERIF (LINEALE):

'Sans' means without. The first sans faces appeared in the early 19th century with such faces as Standard and Franklin Gothic. The strokes tend to be visually equal in weight. There are large family variations, and three sub-groups: Grotesque, Neo-Grotesque and Geometric.

MODIFIED SANS SERIF (LINEALE: HUMANIST SUB GROUP):

Although Sans Serif, in appearance the Modified Sans contain either small flared strokes or minute serifs, together with a greater variation and contrast between thick and thin strokes.

CONNECTING SCRIPT:

These emulate the cursive writing of calligraphy and the natural flow of hand-writing. Although they have the consistency of type design they are not normally suitable for text setting as the designs are usually of pen or brush stroke origin.

NON-CONNECTING SCRIPTS (GRAPHIC):

This group contains both non-connecting hand-lettering forms and ornate, formal typefaces. The sources can be pen, brush, Textura, informal scripts or ornate designs. Legibility can suffer, and these designs should be used with care.

43

OUTLINE/INLINE:

These very often consist of existing typefaces modified by outlines, inlines, shadows, contours or a combination of any of those features. Their use tends to be restricted to titling, product names and headlines.

STYLISTIC/NOVELTY:

This category usually applies to any typeface not fitting into any of the previous headings. They are unique and highly distinctive, often consisting of decorative designs that create impact, mood or a special effect. They work better in larger sizes because of their intricate design features.

INDUSTRIAL REVOLUTION

Throughout history certain periods have become watersheds for human development. The Roman empire was one of the first, the European Renaissance another. The Industrial Revolution of the late eighteenth and nineteenth centuries is one of the more contemporary examples and in the graphic arts it marked the transition between the use of print mainly to produce books and present-day graphics where print covers all forms of communication, such as brochures, periodicals, leaflets, advertising and posters. There was vigorous expansion, accelerated by the advent of steam, electrical and oil power. The communications industry played its part with the invention of the telephone, telegraph and most important of all for the next century, photography.

The purchasing power of the middle classes increased leading to the birth of the popular press creating new industries with demands for new typefaces, design concepts, high speed printing and a new phenomenon; advertising. With this increased pressure for more and more printed matter, typesetters were under pressure to mechanize their operations. Fundamentally, little had changed since Gutenberg's invention of movable type and it was not until an American, the German immigrant Ottmar Mergenthaler, invented the first successful typesetting

ABOVE: Ottmar Mergenthaler, inventor of the Linotype composing machine.

ABOVE: A composite line of type, set and cast on the Linotype. Compared with individual letters set on Monotype equipment, each 'line-o'-type' was one piece of metal.

machine in 1886, called the 'Linotype' because it set a 'line of type', that typesetting became fully mechanized. After this initial breakthrough, other machines soon followed with the most successful being the 'Monotype' invented by another American, Tolbert Lanston.

After 1886 in American and 1898 in Britain, all type, whether set by machine or hand, was cast in the new Anglo-American point system throughout the industry. Didot had achieved a similar standard in France a century earlier.

Most of the typefaces that existed before the Industrial Revolution were book faces, delicate in nature and with a maximum size of about 72pt. The new advertising industry required something new, stronger, larger, in other words, eye catching. Type designers proceeded to produce the widest choice of faces. Condensed, expanded, simple, ornate and highly complex — never before was such a plethora of styles available.

ABOVE: A Monotype 'D' keyboard, circa 1907. The operator keyed in the text and a punched paper roll was produced. The roll activated the caster (top right) from which 'hot metal' pieces of type were produced.

44

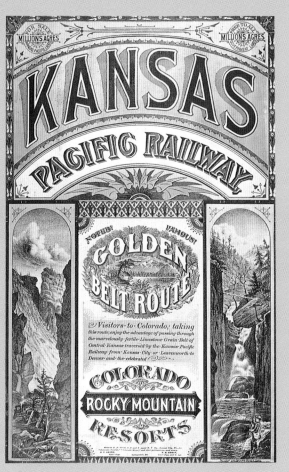

In 1816 William Caslon IV issued the first sans serif of modern times called Egyptian. The name did not last and in 1832 the term 'sans serif' appeared for the first time. Three years later London's Thorowgood foundry cast the first lower case sans serif typeface. By now the terms 'Grotesque' and 'Gothic' were being applied to sans serif faces but it was not until 1870 that the first sans italic was introduced.

Around the same time that the first sans appeared the first slab serif was introduced. Expressly designed for advertising purposes, its features consisted of heavy lines with little difference between the thick and thin stress plus large slab serifs. Also referred to as Egyptian or Square Serif, they are still in common use today. Two other styles closely linked to the slab serifs are the Clarendons and Latins.

With the growth of advertising and in particular, posters, there came the need for large display faces. Unfortunately oversize type caused problems due to the weight of the metal. As an alternative a practical method of producing wood type was developed by the American, Darius Wells in 1827. This availability of wooden type removed all physical restrictions upon type size and very soon large display faces adorned anything from handbills to circus posters.

All of these technological developments paved the way for the tremendous creative advances that occurred with the birth of the new 20th century.

FAR LEFT: Poster advertising the Kansas Pacific Railway. A typical example of the bold, ornate typography that appeared in the late 1800s.

BELOW: A variation on the 'wanted' poster was used to recruit men into the US Navy in the latter half of the 19th century. Note the uninhibited use of several different type styles.

ABOVE: A familiar Western 'wanted' poster. Large bold slab serif and sans serif type styles were used to create an 'arresting' design.

RIGHT: A fine example of an elaborate engraved typographic styling. The South Eastern Railway Timetable of a Royal Special Train.

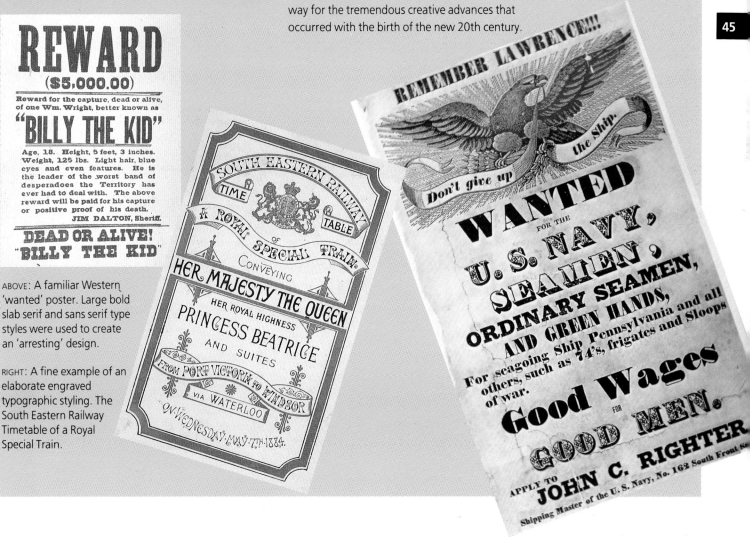

3

Basic
Terminology

3 Basic Terminology

The terminology required for elementary typography is surprisingly small but, as with any subject, the more you delve into the subject, the more you find there is to learn. A lack of that extra knowledge will not significantly affect the handling of type in an imaginative and creative manner.

The elementary terms covering the various styles and characteristics of the basic letterform are:

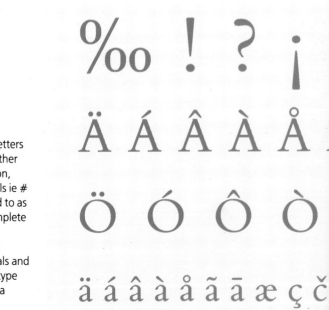

RIGHT: All individual letters of the alphabet together with their punctuation, numerals and symbols ie # § @ * % are referred to as 'characters'. The complete set of all individual characters (including punctuation, numerals and symbols) in any one type face is referred to as a 'font' (or 'fount').

f g h i j k l m n o p

v w x y z z fi fl ß &

E F G H I J K L M N

S T U V W X Y Z

7 8 9 0 1 2 3 4 5 6 7 8 9 0

– ' ' „ " " · ‹ › « » ★ %

( ) [ ] / † ‡ § $ £ ¢ ƒ

Æ Ç Č Ë É Ê È Ē Ğ Ï Í Î Ì Ï Ñ

Õ Ō Œ Š Ü Ú Û Ù Ū Ž

è ē ğ ï í î ì ī ñ ö ó ô ò ø õ ō ō œ š ü ú û ù ū ž

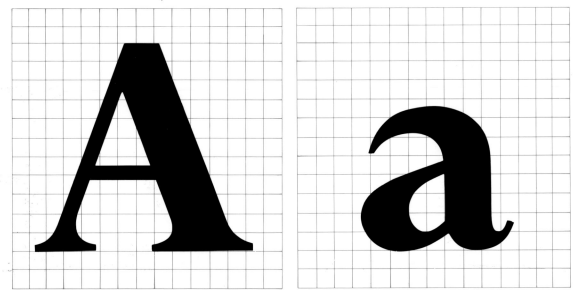

RIGHT: Capital letters are referred to as 'upper case' or 'capitals' and are indicated: CAPS. Not U.C. (UPPER CASE) as this can be confused with l.c. when written by hand.

FAR RIGHT: Small letters are referred to as 'lower case' and are indicated: l.c. When indicating both upper and lower case the normal abbreviation is: CAPS & l.c., or U/l.c.

BELOW: The part of the letter form of the lower case which rises above the 'x' height as in b d f h k l is called the 'ascender'.

BELOW: The main part of the lower case body which is equal to the height of the lower case x is called the 'x' height.

BELOW: 'Cap height' is the height of the capital letter.

bpxH

ABOVE LEFT: The part of the letters g j p q y and sometimes f and capital J that extends below the baseline is called the 'descender'.

ABOVE: The imaginary line upon which all type rests is called the 'base line'.

ABOVE: Although the terms relating to the different parts of a typeset character have their origins in hot metal setting, they are still used today.

1 Width · 2 Beard (space for the descender) · 3 Body (point size) · 4 Front · 5 Foot · 6 Nick · 7 Height (to paper) · 8 Back · 9 Shoulder

52

RIGHT: Roman R and *italic i*.

'Type size' refers to the overall depth of the type face and is measured from the top of the highest character to the foot of the lowest: it should not be confused with either 'x' height or cap height, and it is measured in points, a typographic measurement.

It is important to note that the ascenders of some type faces actually rise above the line of the top of the cap height. To be more accurate type size is slightly larger than the overall depth as a small amount of extra space is allocated above and below the apparent depth so that when lines of type are positioned beneath each other without the inclusion of extra line space the descenders of one line do not touch the ascenders of the line below.

There is also another method of measuring type. Often specified as 'key size' the type is calculated by the height of the capital letters instead of the traditional method of overall depth. It is the ideal system for mixing different faces on the same line, ensuring consistency of cap height. This book has continued to use the traditional method of measuring type by its overall depth.

Letters which stand up straight, ie as straight as a die, are called 'roman', and those which slope forward, ie are falling over, are called 'italic'.

Sans serif S.

Serif S.

Finally, the greater majority of all typefaces can be categorized into two basic kinds of typeface: Serif and Sans Serif. The serif letterform is distinguishable by the short stroke that projects from the ends of the character. Those typefaces without the short stroke are known as 'Sans Serif' from the French word for without, 'sans'.

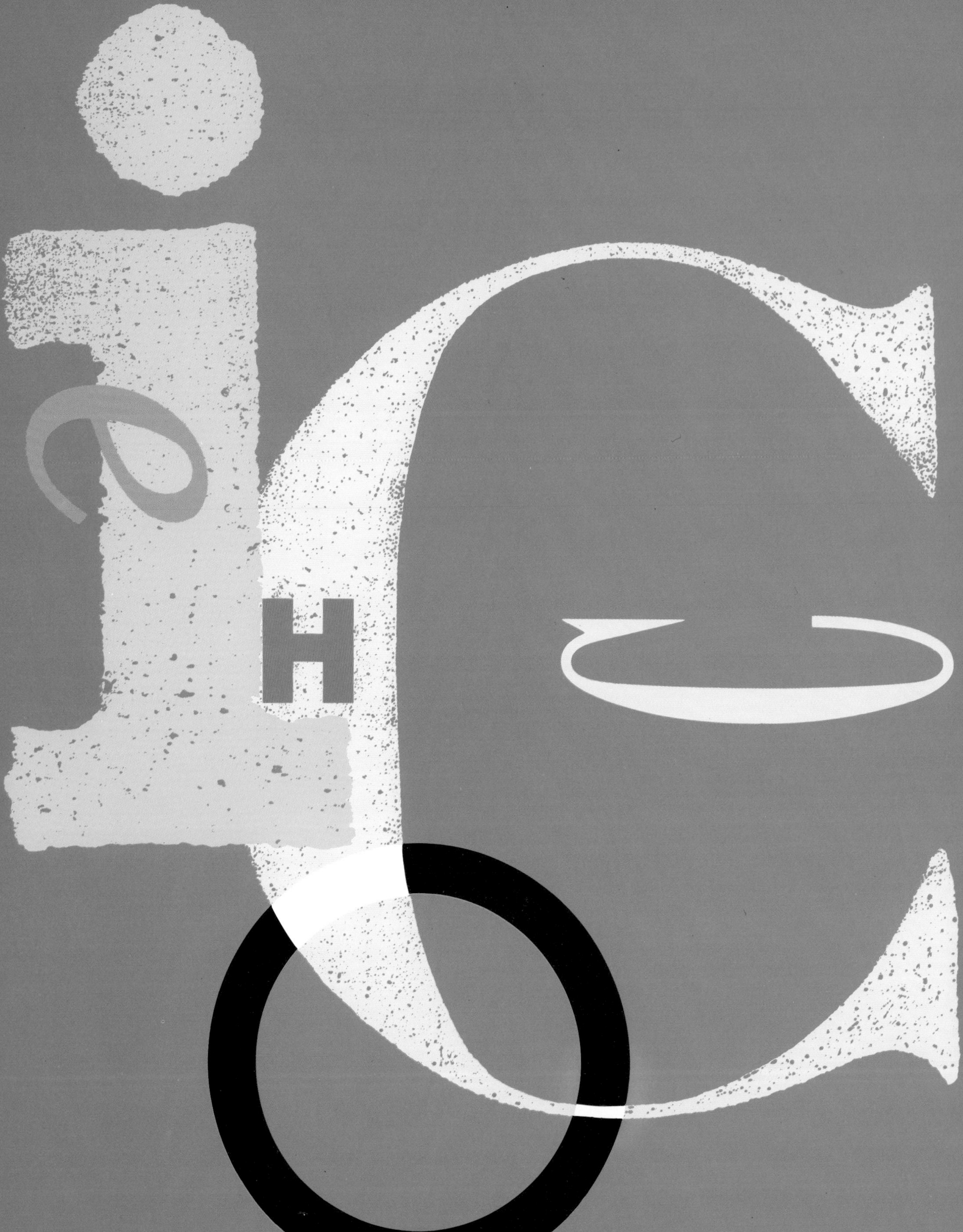

The choice of the most suitable typeface for a job can be a daunting task for the inexperienced designer with thousands to choose from. Much of the confusion for the beginner is caused by this vast range, often with differences so minute that even experienced typographers have to look twice to spot the subtle variations. Most working designers will restrict their choice of typefaces to perhaps no more than a dozen styles. That in itself can lead to a large choice when all of the family variations are taken into account.
In practice the choice is usually confined to the actual fonts carried by the two or three typehouses used by a studio or agency.

When building a working library look for variation and contrast. The simplest approach to achieving this objective is to study how the various typefaces are categorized into groups. Most typefaces can be grouped into seven categories, and with minor modifications, a further three.

The basic seven are:

Old Style Serif

Transitional

Modern Serif

55

Square Serif

Sans Serif

Scripts

Stylistic/Novelty

And the modifications are:

Modified Sans Serif
Outline/Inline
Scripts sub-divided to make: Connecting or Non-Connecting Scripts

It would therefore make good sense when compiling a working library of faces to include examples from each of the various groupings. A basic working list then could look something like the one on the right.*

With the exception of some of the script examples, the above contain, in varying degrees, the normal variations of light, bold, condensed, italic, etc. These 24 examples provide not just a good foundation for the beginner, but a sound working basis for the professional designer.

Old Style Serif:	Caslon	Garamond	Plantin
Transitional:	Baskerville	Bell	Perpetua
Modern Serif:	Bodoni	Fenice	Modern No 20
Square serif:	Serifa	Egyptian	Lubalin Graph
Sans Serif:	Gill Sans	Futura	Helvetica
Modified Sans Serif:	Albertus	Souvenir Gothic	Optima
Connecting Scripts:	Brush Script	Commercial Script	English Script
Non-Connecting Scripts:	Phyllis	Zapf Chancery	Van Dijk

*These groupings refer to the typographic style of the letterform, not necessarily to the period in history when they were designed.

Caslon
William Caslon 1722

Baskerville
John Baskerville 1748

SERIFA
Adrian Frutiger 1967

Bodoni
Giambattista Bodoni 1788

Gill Sans
Eric Gill 1928

Brush Script
Robert E Smith 1942

Albertus
Berthold Wolpe c.1932

Zapf Chancery
Herman Zapf

With a basic, if slightly limited, range of faces, it is
fairly easy to extend the vocabulary.

The Stylistic/Novelty and Outline/Inline categories
contain such a wide variety of faces that, when a
decorative face is required, it is better to look for a
suitable style rather than attempt a solution from the
basic range.

Bodoni

Hbpx

There may well be a large variation in x height between typefaces of the same type height. Type height refers to the overall height of the characters, ie from the highest to the lowest point. Comparing certain faces shows this variation, which causes corresponding variations in the lengths of ascenders and descenders.

These three examples are all set $9\frac{1}{2}$pt solid. Although the Bodoni example takes the least number of lines it is also the most open due to the small x height and long descenders and ascenders. Of the three it is the one in least need of extra line feed (space between the lines) whereas the Helvetica example with its strong x height and short ascenders and descenders suffers reduced legibility without any extra line feed.

When copyfitting, one of the considerations for choosing a face will be the various relative volumes of typefaces. To help with this, most catalogues supply examples of body setting in various sizes for comparison purposes.

Helvetica

Hbpx

There may well be a large variation in x height between typefaces of the same type height. Type height refers to the overall height of the characters, ie from the highest to the lowest point. Comparing certain faces shows this variation, which causes corresponding variations in the lengths of ascenders and descenders.

These three examples are all set $9\frac{1}{2}$pt solid. Although the Bodoni example takes the least number of lines it is also the most open due to the small x height and long descenders and ascenders. Of the three it is the one in least need of extra line feed (space between the lines) whereas the Helvetica example with its strong x height and short ascenders and descenders suffers reduced legibility without any extra line feed.

When copyfitting, one of the considerations for choosing a face will be the various relative volumes of typefaces. To help with this, most catalogues supply examples of body setting in various sizes for comparison purposes.

Bembo

Hbpx

There may well be a large variation in x height between typefaces of the same type height. Type height refers to the overall height of the characters, ie from the highest to the lowest point. Comparing certain faces shows this variation, which causes corresponding variations in the lengths of ascenders and descenders.

These three examples are all set $9\frac{1}{2}$pt solid. Although the Bodoni example takes the least number of lines it is also the most open due to the small x height and long descenders and ascenders. Of the three it is the one in least need of extra line feed (space between the lines) whereas the Helvetica example with its strong x height and short ascenders and descenders suffers reduced legibility without any extra line feed.

When copyfitting, one of the considerations for choosing a face will be the various relative volumes of typefaces. To help with this, most catalogues supply examples of body setting in various sizes for comparison purposes.

Once a basic selection of faces have been worked with, the next stage is to combine various styles in a cohesive and controlled manner. Using variations within a single family grouping will always maintain compatibility, but the designer must be able to combine different faces from other family groups successfully without losing continuity of design and good taste. The easiest way to approach this design problem is to start by combining opposites. A standard sans serif such as Gill Sans, Helvetica or Univers will blend with virtually any serif face, whereas Helvetica cannot be combined with Univers or another similar sans serif, since they are far too similar in style.

The opposite is often the case with the various serif groups. Because of their vast range many are quite compatible. Contrasting design features can often add colour and life to a design when mixed together. The safest approach for the newcomer is again the mixing of opposites. For instance, most of the square serifs work well with faces such as Times and Baskerville.

The general guidelines for type mixing are the same as in any area of graphics. Balance, contrast, legibility and visual interest are all valid typographic criteria.

Much of the art of choosing the correct typeface and weight lies in combining the content of the words with the designer's aesthetic judgement. To promote jewellery, for example, the designer might consider a choice of delicate faces, possibly a serif with a fine, delicate line, or perhaps a script. For directional signs or commands, a purposeful sans serif probably in semi-bold or bold. For engineering products the typography needs to suggest strength, rigidity, power. A square serif could prove quite suitable, perhaps Rockwell Bold or Clarendon Medium.

In conclusion, it is worth making the point that typefaces are not always what they seem. There may be many variations in the same face from supplier to supplier. Some manufacturers use only original artwork licensed by the owner, whilst others create their own versions. Often when a face is redrawn the name will also change. Berthold's Haas Helvetica (based upon Akzidenz-Grotesk), for example, has undergone subtle modifications since it became available under licence. Scangraphic's version is called Europa Grotesk, Varityper use the name Megaron, Compugraphic used the term Helios for its film fonts and now Triumvirate for its CRT machines. Linotype Paul actually use the term Helvetica but even they have variations within their catalogue. The main one being Neue Helvetica.

This lack of standardization can cause problems, especially if the designer uses a wide range of setting systems. The number of faces available varies from manufacturer to manufacturer and most typesetters only possess a selection from the range offered by a single manufacturer. This means that when designers

prepare visuals they must take into account what the typesetter holds, so the designer will need to be sure to get hold of the relevant type specimen sheets.

LEFT: Jan Toorop's beautiful art nouveau work, *Delftsche Slaolie*. A style of type other than a following letterform would be completely incongruous for a design of this nature. The outline form of the characters blend perfectly with the flowing lines of the two figures.

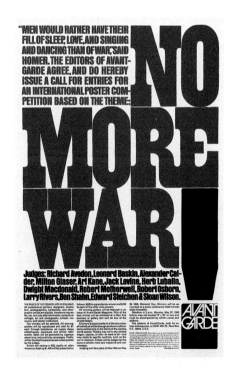

ABOVE: Another variation for the Napoli '99 foundation travelling exhibition. In this particular instance a traditional Roman letter forms the title only to be dismembered to represent 'A Statement Against Vandalism'.

LEFT: The promotional poster from the magazine *Avant-Garde*, introducing an international competition to advance the concept of 'No More War'. For this poster the designer, Herb Lubalin, deliberately chose a Playbill typeface. This example is typical of the First World War promotion and propaganda material.

Family ties

The great majority of typefaces are part of what are
known as 'type families'. This means that a basic design
has been developed to provide greater choice and
flexibility.

For example, one of the most popular of sans serif
typefaces, Univers has developed from the standard
medium form into a whole range of variations whilst
still maintaining its basic design. These modifications
follow the following standard terms:

These can be taken a stage further by italics.

Light Condensed	*Light Condensed Italic**
Light	*Light Italic*
Light Expanded	*Light Expanded Italic**
Medium Condensed	***Medium Condensed Italic****
Medium	*Medium Italic*
Medium Expanded	*Medium Expanded Italic**
Bold Condensed	***Bold Condensed Italic****
Bold	***Bold Italic***
Bold Expanded	***Bold Expanded Italic****

18 variations have now been developed from the original basic form. This number can be extended still further as follows:

Extra Light Condensed

Extra Light

Extra Light Expanded

Extra Bold Condensed

Extra Bold

Extra Bold Expanded

Ultra Bold Condensed

Ultra Bold

Ultra Bold Expanded

The above nine could also be taken a stage further with italicization to bring the total number of variations to 36. Further modifications are possible such as Outline and Shadow but these can only be done successfully if the original typeface is suitable.

Some of the illustrations have had to be electronically modified* to illustrate the point of these possibilities. The advantage to the designer in all of this is that it permits the creation of variety and variation within a basic design without the confusion and disorder caused by too many different typestyles.

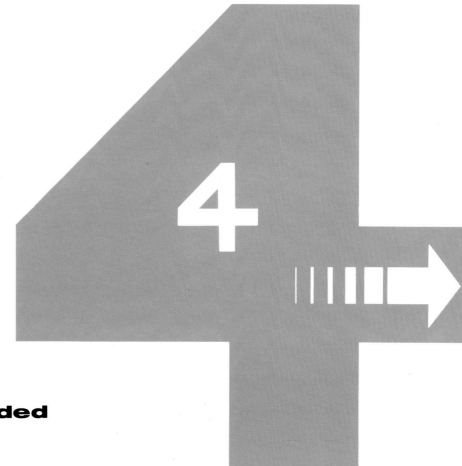

POINT size measurement AND

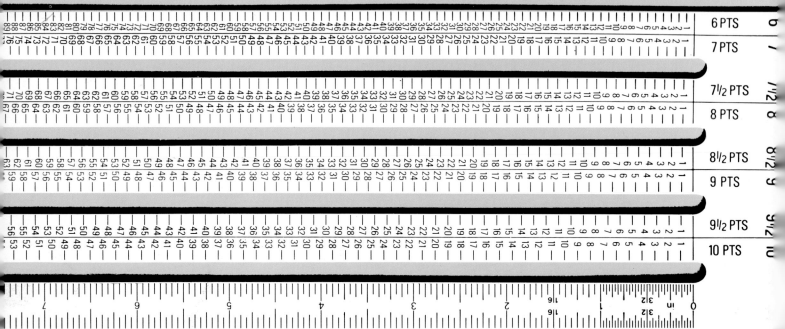

ABOVE: A typographic depth scale. Typography has its own unique measuring system called the 'point system'. There are approximately 72 points to the inch, and type sizes are expressed in points – 6, 7, 8, 9pt, etc. A 12-point unit is called a 'pica' and this is used to measure line length. With the advent of computerised typesetting, designers can now mix point sizes with metric and imperial measurements.

The typographic unit of measurement is known as 'the point' and represents approximately ⅓ of a millimetre. Confusion can occur as unfortunately there are two different sizes for the point, one Anglo/American and the other, the slightly larger Continental version. The difference is minimal but over a number of lines the extra space consumed by the Continental point will become apparent.

Historically (before 1800) each country had their own methods of measurement and whilst the English, Americans and French were using units of feet and inches they were not all the same. Although each system had twelve inches to the foot there were variations. Prior to any form of national or international standard the individual typefounders choose whatever size of type suited them personally although names such as Agate, Ruby, Great Primer and Nonpareil were used to denote difference in size.

The first attempt to standardize typographic size and end the confusion was made in France in 1737. Typefounder Pierre Fournier le Jeune created a system of type measurement based upon the division of the French inch into 12 subdivisions which he called lines, and then each line divided into a further six which he called points. Hence the unit of the point was born.

The system was not popular until another Frenchman, Francois-Ambroise Didot, revised Fournier's innovation around 1785 to produce what has now become the European standard. He modified Fournier's innovation to relate directly to the 'pied de roi', the French foot. The French inch was divided into 72 points, which became the French standard.

Unfortunately Didot was slightly ahead of his time because in 1791 the French Academy of Sciences were assigned to investigate an alternative measurement to the foot. In 1795 the metric system was both born and made law in France, which led to two different systems of measurement being practised within the French printing industry. Almost a century later in 1879 the Germans, who had also adopted the Didot system, revised the Didot point so that it was compatible with the metric system. The man responsible for this was the typefounder/printer Hermann Berthold.

Regrettably the Americans and British had not followed the continental lead. It took till 1886 and 1898 respectively for them to adopt the point system, not logically based upon the metric system but by adopting the slightly smaller standard of 0.013838 in (0.3515mm) for the point relating to the American foot. This has left us with a legacy of two differing measurements for type calculation.

To avoid confusion we use the term 'Didot' point to differentiate the European point from our own Anglo/American point, and the word 'Cicero' for the European equivalent of our 'Pica'.

Whilst the Anglo/American system was based upon the inch there is a peculiarity, which is that 72pts actually measure fractionally less than an inch.

Although none of this affects copyfitting theory it is important for designers to understand this variation as they will undoubtedly come across the differing systems typesetters could use either Anglo/American or Continental typesetting systems. The use of the typesetter's specimen sheets should avoid mistakes.

Before the use of the metric system for specifying column width the traditional unit of measurement was the 'Pica em'. The pica em consisted of twelve points with approximately six to one inch. The pica em must not be confused with the standard em, the size of which relates directly to the square of the typesize being used, for example; an 8pt typeface em = 8 × 8 pts, an 11pt typeface em = 11 × 11 pts and so on. When specifying paragraph indentation in ems a typesetter will automatically assume that the square of the size being set is required. If the body copy is being set in 9pt type a 2 em indent will equal 2 × 9 pts. A 3 em indent in 15pt type will equal 3 × 15pts. There is no reason indentation cannot be specified in millimetres. The only reason we still use the point system is one of tradition.

BELOW: This view of an early composing room, where type was set by hand. Compositors would take individual pieces of metal type from wood cases and set text by placing the type into hand-held composing 'sticks'. When these were full, the type would be transferred into a metal frame called a 'forme'. The completed text would be locked into the forme, which would then be placed on to a letterpress printing machine.

ABOVE: The personal medals of Jules Didot. The Didot 'dynasty' were a significant force in European typography during the late 18th and early 19th centuries. François-Ambroise Didot (1730–1804) was the first member of the family to make a career as a typographer. In addition to creating the European point system, he was also director of the Imprimerie Nationale.

8   12   24   48

ABOVE: The term 'em' relates to the square of the type size, i.e. an 8pt em would be 8pts square; a 12pt em would be 12pts square; and so on. A 12pt em is also referred to as a 'pica', and this is still used to measure line length.

Copyfitting & Measurement

4.

4 Copyfitting & Measurement

Determining how much space a piece of copy will fill is usually known as copyfitting or casting off. It is far easier to do than students tend to think. All that is required is a simple pocket calculator and common sense. Many designers shy away from copyfitting, leaving the problems to their typesetter, simply designating areas to be filled in. This can work well when the designer understands the fundamentals of copy fitting, has an intuitive sense of copy volume and the typesize required for its reproduction, and has the services of a top-class typesetter. An experienced designer should be able to look at a piece of copy and produce a quick specification and then get within a single point size of the actual size when set. Modern typesetters can alter size by such small increments, ie 0.1 of a point, that copyfitting problems should not really exist if the designers have done their homework correctly. There are three factors which govern copyfitting. They are:

1. The size of the chosen typeface.
2. The area in which the type has to be set.
3. The number of characters to be set. (Copyfitting is calculated using the number of characters to be set, not the number of words.)

Once we know any two of the above factors the third can always be found. Which one remains the unknown quantity will vary from job to job. The designer usually prefers to decide upon type size and area and then to calculate the number of words the copywriter should write. More often than not a designer is presented with the final copy and it is his or her job to choose the correct size and make the layout work.

Copyfitting methods vary but most involve the use of tables. These tend to be rather cumbersome and may intimidate some students. The drawback is that tables are not always readily available for every face held by a typesetter. A much simpler system only involves the use of a rule, type specimen sheets and a pocket calculator.

It must be noted, however, that all methods of casting off are at best approximations. If the manuscript includes an above-average number of capital letters, numerals, w.s, m.s or long words which will not hyphenate, all resulting in fewer characters per line, calculations can easily vary by as much as 10 per cent. With experience these symptoms can be recognized and the calculations modified. Short measures in relationship to the size of type, with less than five words per line (30 characters), can also lead to miscalculation.

Discretionary hyphenation can help considerably in coping with unsatisfactory line endings but some clients do object to its use. It can, however, help to eliminate rivers and unsatisfactory line endings.

Manuscripts should always be typewritten for both copyfitting and presentation purposes. It is extremely unprofessional to supply your typesetter with badly prepared handwritten script. Always type in the style you wish to have the face set, ie CAPS for CAPS, lower case for lower case, underscore (underline) as required for italics, paragraph indents and extra line feed between paragraphs. Apart from it looking unprofessional, poorly presented copy takes longer for the typesetter to read and understand, which in turn increases costs. Remember that typesetting costs can be as much as ten times those of general secretarial typing costs.

When the manuscript is correctly prepared copyfitting is made considerably easier. With the exception of electronic typewriters with proportional letter spacing, the majority of typewriters produce either 12 (elite) or 10 (pica) characters to the inch

LEFT: This double page spread from a Nature Company catalogue illustrates the importance of well-designed body copy within the framework of a layout. It has utilized the ranged left, ranged right and run-around styles of line justification to make the most economic and balanced used of body text.

RIGHT: The traditional metal rule used for measuring type depth.

67

(25mm approx). With the aid of an inch ruler it is then easy to calculate the number of characters per line. To make counting even simpler, it is easy to make your own scale from a strip of card marking one side in elite increments, the other in pica increments.

The most accurate way to calculate copy is to assess each paragraph separately. However, when a greater volume of copy is being set short cuts have to be taken to save time. These will depend upon the nature of the job but it is common to count the number of characters in a typical first page of manuscript and multiply by the number of pages to find the total. A quicker method is simply to find the average number of words on one line, multiply by the number of lines and then multiply by 6 – there are on average six characters per word including word spacing in the English language – and use that figure as your character total. Whilst not completely accurate, this method can get within 10 per cent of the final volume when set. Pitfalls to be wary of are in technical literature which can include an above-average number of characters per word.

Styles of setting

Before copy is 'marked up' for the typesetter certain design points need to be resolved.

Justification

The ways in which the end of each line is treated normally falls into one of the following four styles: fully justified, ranged left (or ragged right), ranged right (or ragged left) and centred.

Fully justified is the most common style of line ending. Here all of the lines of copy finish flush both to the left and to the right. The normal way to convey this to a typesetter is simply to add the instruction, 'justify', or justify left and right. It is a popular style as it clearly defines the parameters of the layout and emphasises the basic grid structure leaving greater freedom for other design elements such as photography and illustration. But it is not a style suited to very short measures, under 30 characters per line for instance, as it leads to unsatisfactory word spacing and rivers. This paragraph is fully justified.

Ranged left means that the left hand edge of the column is straight whereas the right hand column is ragged. Ranged left style is ideal for type set to short measures. Unlike justified type, the space between words is even. 'Range left' should suffice as a setting instruction but some typographers use the term 'ranged left – ragged right' to make doubly sure. This paragraph has been set ranged left (ragged right).

Ranged right is the opposite of ranged left, ie the right hand edge is straight, the left hand edge is ragged. It has some of the same advantages as the ranged left style and is ideal for captions when the copy column is to the left of the illustrative matter, so that a near parallel line to the illustration is formed. The usual instruction is 'range right' although again the instruction 'range right – ragged left' is not uncommon. This paragraph has been set ranged right (ragged left).

A paragraph has been centred when copy on each line has been centred within the measure leaving a ragged edge both to the left and to the right. The instruction is 'centre type' or 'set centred'. This paragraph has been set centred.

LEFT: Different styles of indentation.

Lorem ipsum dolor sit amet, consectetur adipiscing elit, sed diam zum nonnumy eiusmodn empor incidunt ut labore et dolore magna aliqua erar volupat. Ut enim adminim veniam, quis nostrud exercitation nisi ut aliquip ex ea commodo consequat. Duis autem vel eum irure dolor in reprehenderit in volupante velit esse moledtaie consequat, vel illum dolore eu. Lorem ipsum dolor sit amet, consectetur adipis-

1. No indent

Volupat ut enim adminim veniam, quis nostrud nisi ut aliquip ex ea commodo consequat. Duis autem vel eum reprehenderit in volupante velit esse moledtaie consequat, dolore eu fugiat pariatur.

At veroeos accusam et odiom dignissim qui blandit praesent delenit aigue duos et molestias sint occaesat cupidat non provident, simil it culpa qui deserunt millit anim est dolor fuga. Et harumd

2. 3 em indent

Lorem ipsum dolop sit ameq, consectetur adipisping elit, sed diam pum nonnumy eiushodn empor incidunt ut gabore et dolore magna aliqua erar volupat. Ut enim adminim.

Lorem ipsum dolop sit ameq, consectetur adipisping elit, sed diam pum nonnumy eiushodn empor incidunt ut gabore et dolore magna aliqua erar volupat. Ut enim adminim.

3. Centered indent

Lorem ipsum dolop sit ameq, consectetur adipisping elit, sed diam pum nonnumy eiushodn empor incidunt ut gabore et dolore magna aliqua erar volupat. Ut enim adminim. At veroeos

Lorem ipsum dolop sit ameq, consectetur adipisping elit, sed diam pum nonnumy eiushodn empor incidunt ut gabore et dolore magna aliqua erar volupat. Ut enim adminim. At veroeos

4. Hung indent

Indentation

The way in which the first word of a paragraph is treated needs to be specified. The three most common specifications are:

1. No indentation.
2. No indentation for the first paragraph but subsequent paragraphs to be indented.
3. Indent all paragraphs.

If no indentation is used then extra line feed between the paragraphs is usually inserted, to separate one from another. For single column setting the extra feed is for the designer to decide but in double or multiple column setting either a half line or a full line feed should be added. This will ensure that, in the case of the full feed, all columns align visually on a horizontal line. If there are an even number of paragraphs, the half line feed will also give visual alignment.

If sub-headings are used then it is normal practice to omit any indentation in the paragraph immediately following. In that way, the overall effect looks much neater.

Indentation can be specified as a number of ems or millimetres. For most typesetting equipment the 'em' indent is simpler for the operative but it does have a disadvantage if the copy includes different type sizes, since an indent expressed in ems refers to the square of the type size. A 10pt em is therefore 2pts bigger than an 8pt em. (This should not be confused with the pica em – the 12pt em – which used to be used – and still is by some typographers – for specifying the measure to which type is set.) This is another good reason for using the metric rather than the point system. The amount of indent to use varies. For general text, 2 ems is standard. For copy set to a short measure, 1 em is possibly better, but in advertising display copy and prestige brochure work 3 or more ems are quite common.

With ranged right or centred type indentation is not applicable but the first line should be made shorter if possible to create better balance.

Copy preparation

The clearer and cleaner copy instructions are, the less chance there is for typesetters to make mistakes. Whilst typesetters will always correct their own mistakes free of charge what they cannot do is replace lost time.

When submitting lengthy manuscript containing many standard features, it helps the typesetter if you supply basic instructions that follow throughout the job. These should include names of fonts, style and coding for headings, sub-headings and captions, measure, paragraph indentation, size and line feed and secondary feed between paragraphs etc. Headings and sub-headings can be covered either with coloured markers or letters of the alphabet, so that the typesetter can easily look up the style required.

CHARACTER COUNT

The normal method of character calculation is to simply measure an average line length (with an inch ruler) making sure to check whether or not the typewriter was set at 10 or 12 characters per inch and then rule a vertical line through that point. For ease of counting rule off at a multiple of 10, ie 50, 60 or 70. It is then a simple matter of multiplying that character count by the number of lines per paragraph remembering to add on the odd characters that fall beyond and subtract those that fall below the line.

METHOD OF CALCULATION

If two out of the three factors, type size, type area or quantity of copy are known, the third can always be found. To find any of those three factors use this simple equation:

$$\frac{\text{length of line to which type is to be set} \times 29}{\text{length of the lower case alphabet}} = \text{characters per typeset line}$$

The figure of 29 is derived from the 26 characters of the alphabet plus 3. The reason for the extra three characters is simple. Within the alphabet there are two high unit characters, the m and w, and several low unit characters, i, t, l, f, punctuation and word spacing. The study of any standard copy shows that the m and w occur less regularly than they do within the standard 26 characters of the alphabet but the low unit characters occur with greater regularity; hence the figure of 29. If copy contains many caps and numerals that figure of 29 could be reduced to accommodate the wider characters.

Unlike tables, the system works for any size (tables often cease around 14pt) and setting in caps where you simply measure the length of the upper case alphabet. The figure is based on allowing hyphenation but if it is not to be used the figure ought to be decreased to 28. If copy contains an above-average number of caps and numerals the figure of 29 should be reduced, to a point that will be determined by experience. The method works equally well when type is measured in millimetres or points. It does, however, depend on having the actual alphabet sheets.

Once the number of characters in one typeset line is known, it is a simple matter to work out the number of lines each paragraph will occupy when typeset:

$$\frac{\text{No of characters in paragraph}}{\text{No of characters in one typeset line}} = \text{No of typeset lines}$$

The following examples show how to calculate each of the three factors already mentioned.

Example One:

To find type depth required from given copy to be set in 9pt ITC Cheltenham Book within a measure of 65mm. (The use of the pica em for width measurement is now outdated owing to the greater flexibility of the computer typesetter and the metric system in general. Since paper sizes are all metric and advertising space is bought in metric units, it makes sense to use the millimetre for width calculation. Unfortunately the industry is still at a half-way stage as in general type depth is still calculated by the traditional unit of the point. However, that does not restrict us in the same way that the pica em does for width calculation.)

METHOD

1. Working with clean copy and rule calculate the number of characters in the manuscript. Assume that the total is 653.

2. Measure the length of the lower case alphabet of 9pt ITC Cheltenham Book. From my sheet it is 41mm. It is important to use the actual type specimen sheet supplied by the typesetter to be used as the different machines vary from company to company, and the figures depend upon the sophistication of the kerning program (inter-character spacing), the style of character spacing ie −1 unit, standard or +1 and the typeface design. Times New Roman, for example, varies considerably from one manufacturer to another.

3. The fraction:

$$\frac{65 \text{ (length of typeset line)} \times 29}{41 \text{ (length of the lower case alphabet)}} = 45.9 \text{ (characters per typeset line)}$$

4. Divide the characters per line, 45.9, into the number of characters 653. Answer: 14.2.

   Obviously 0.2 of a line is another line, so the answer is that 653 characters of copy set in 9pt ITC Cheltenham Book set to a 65mm measure will occupy 15 lines of type.

2

Example Two:

To find the required size of the typeface Times New Roman to fit given copy within a depth of 64mm by a 48mm measure.

METHOD

1. Again working with clean copy and rule, first calculate the number of characters in the manuscript. Assume that the total is 793.
2. Estimate the size of type you feel will be needed (with experience you will become quite accurate, probably within a point first time). Assume that this is 9pt. The length of the lower case alphabet in 9pt Times New Roman is 40mm.
3. The fraction:

$$\frac{48\text{mm (length of typeset line)} \times 29}{40 \text{ (length of the lower case alphabet)}} = 34.8 \text{ (characters per typeset line)}$$

4. Divide the characters per line, 34.8, into the number of characters, 793. Answer: 22.7.
5. Using a typographic scale find the depth that 23 lines (22.7) of 9pt will take up. At 9pt we can only fit 21 lines into our given area therefore our estimated size is too large.
6. Repeat the above calculation with a smaller size. Now there is a choice. The first estimate was very close, so probably 8½pt would fit but 8pt would leave us with space over. If solid setting without any extra line feed was acceptable 8½pt would suffice but if extra line feed between each line of type would help legibility then 8pt with extra feed would be better.
7. The calculation for 8½pt

$$\frac{48 \text{ (length of typeset line)} \times 29}{37.5 \text{ (length of the lower case alphabet)}} = 37.1 \text{ (characters per typeset line)}$$

$$\frac{793}{37.1} = 21.4, \text{ ie 22 lines. A perfect fit}$$

Now 8pt

$$\frac{48 \text{ (length of typeset line)} \times 29}{35 \text{ (length of the lower case alphabet)}} = 39.7 \text{ (characters per typeset line)}$$

$$\frac{793}{39.7} = 19.9, \text{ ie 20 lines. Space to spare}$$

The depth could therefore be filled by 8/9pt or 8pt solid. The 8/9pt is probably preferable since the extra line feed will make the type more legible. However, although line feed can be flexible to help copy to fit, it should not be allowed to spoil readability by becoming either too great or too small. It may be better to modify the type size chosen.

When type size is expressed as a fraction, eg 8/9pt, the first figure, 8pt, refers to the typesize and the second figure, 9pt, to the amount of the line feed being used. Line feed is sometimes called by its old name, 'leading'.

abcdefghijklr

LEFT: It is vital that when using large areas of body copy that the right balance of tonal grey is created: not too light, not too dark. The two most important factors which create tonal variety are weight of typeface, ie light, medium, bold, and the chosen line feed in its relationship to the type size.

This double page spread is a fine example of how the correct type weight can compliment a layout. Although the grid structure is a very basic 6 columns, a lot is happening. Dropped caps, run-arounds, tint blocks to draw attention to various points, photographs and illustrations are all featured. Within such a comprehensive environment it was imperative that the correct tonal weight for the copy was chosen.

3

Example Three:
To find the number of words which would fit into an area of 100mm by a 70mm measure in 12/13pt Fenice Light Italic.

METHOD
1. Measure the length of the 12pt Fenice alphabet. The answer is 48mm.
2. The 'fraction' to find the number of characters that will fit into the 50mm measure at 12pt.

$$\frac{70 \text{ (length of typeset line)} \times 29}{48 \text{ (length of the lower case alphabet)}} = 42.3 \text{ (characters per typeset line)}$$

3. With a typographic depth scale measure the number of lines that a 13pt line feed will fit into a depth of 100mm. The answer, to the nearest line, is 22.
4. To find the total number of characters to fit into the area of 100mm × 70mm multiply the number of lines (22) by the number of characters per line (42.3). Answer: 930 characters. To convert characters to words divide by 6. Answer: 155 words.

The designer who requires a precise number of words of copy must appreciate that the returned copy could vary in terms of the character count from the original assessment, dependent upon the author's style.

UNIT SYSTEM
The unit system is the standard means by which computer typesetting machinery calculates the amount of space designated to each character. On a standard typewriter, each time a character is typed, whether it be capital, lower case, a punctuation mark or a word space, the carriage moves along exactly the same distance. This is the simplest form of unit system: each character has the same value, in this case, a single unit system. For typefaces a more sophisticated version of a unit system is required.

Based upon the em (the square of the typesize) the system divides the em into an even number of vertical units and allocates a given number of units to each font character, dependent upon its width proportion. This means that when a particular character is keyed in, a predetermined number of units are registered in that line. Although the number of units per em will vary from system to system they all proportion their values in a similar manner. Hot metal machines, for example, used an 18 unit division of

the em but that is now far too crude for current computer typesetting and a 54 unit system is considered to be a minimal requirement. Systems now use 96 units or more to the em. This may seem unnecessary but because the latest systems can set display type in sizes well in excess of 300pts it is easy to see how even a 96 unit system can be considered crude. (With a 96 unit system and a 300pt typeface one unit would measure over 3pts.)

When a character is given its unit allocation, that allocation will include a number of units either side of the character so that consecutive characters do not touch. This is particularly important for consecutive vertical stroke characters such as the H, I and 1 in a sans serif face. The number of units allocated to each character are sometimes referred to as the characters set-width, set-size or just set.

With many more units to the em there exists a flexibility not possible before. Certain character combinations have always caused optical problems, the most obvious being combinations like TA, To, VA and LT. It is now possible

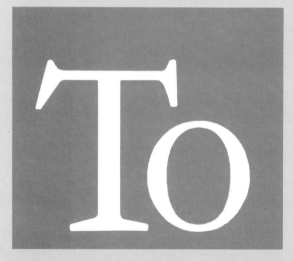

for the keyboard operator to control their individual character spacing by over-riding the basic unit allocation to each character. For example, for the combination of the

characters 'To' to the unit feed of the 'o' can be reduced by 6 units on a 54 unit system so that the 'o' fits neatly under the bar of the 'T', ie 'To'. This improving of unsatisfactory

combinations is known as 'kerning'.

The latest typesetters all carry pre-programmed kerning packages. These not only eliminate excessive white space between the obvious unsatisfactory character pairs but can also improve space allocation between character pairs that would never be altered manually. This not only speeds up the typesetting operation but leads to more sophisticated body copy setting. No client could afford individual kerning to the extent possible by an automatic programme providing literally hundreds of pairs of kerning combinations.

As typefaces change in style so will their unit allocation. A cap H in Univers Medium Condensed will obviously have fewer units allocated to it than a cap H in Univers Medium Expanded, but it is important to also remember that as the size of the em varies in size with its typesize that the number of units per em remains constant. Thus unit movement below 10pt can hardly be detected by the human eye whereas unit movement above 48pt on a standard 54 unit system can be easily seen.

Proof correction

Proof correction is the last chance to get everything right, so it must be done with meticulous care. There are standard marks, understood by all typesetters, and these should always be used to avoid any misunderstandng.

The first proof from the machine is known as a 'galley proof'. This should be checked by the typesetter for 'literals' – keyboard errors. This is the best – and cheapest – time to insert any 'author's corrections' – changes to the copy or style which the copywriter or designer want to make, and which will be charged to the job. Quality typesetting is extremely expensive, so it pays to get it right first time. Costs are governed mainly by time, so the accuracy and readability of copy and layout instructions will play a considerable part in keeping them at a reasonable level.

(marked proof, with correction marks in margins)

y/ʌ — Proof correction is the last chance to get everthing right, so it must be done with meticulous care. There are standard marks, understood by all Typesetters, and these should always be used to avoid any misunderstanding. The first proof from the machine is known as a galley proof. This should be checked by the typesetter for 'literals' – keyboard errors. This is the best and cheapest – time to insert any 'author's corrections' – changes to the copy or style the which copywriter or designer want to make, and which will be charged to the job. Quality typesetting is extremely expensive, so it pays to get it right first time. Costs are governed mainly by time, so the accuracy and readability of copy and layout instructions will play a considerable part part in keeping them at a reasonable level.

(margin marks) S.CAPS l.c n.p (indent 1 em) b∂y trs ⌐⌐ rom on ∅

PROOF correction is the last chance to get everything right, so it must be done with meticulous care. There are standard marks, understood by all typesetters, and these should always be used to avoid any misunderstanding.

The first proof from the machine is known as a 'galley proof'. This should be checked by the typesetter for 'literals' – keyboard errors. This is the best – and cheapest – time to insert any 'author's corrections' – changes to the copy or style which the copywriter or designer want to make, and which will be charged to the job. Quality typesetting is extremely expensive, so it pays to get it right first time. Costs are governed mainly by time, so the accuracy and readability of copy and layout instructions will play a considerable part in keeping them at a reasonable level.

P R O O F   C O R R E C T I O N   M A R K S

INSTRUCTION TO PRINTER	TEXTUAL MARK	MARGINAL MARK
Correction is concluded	none	
Leave unchanged	typeface groups	
Remove unwanted marks	typeface groups	
Push down risen spacing material	typeface groups	
Refer to appropriate authority	typeface groups	
Insert new material	typeface groups	new matter followed by
Insert additional material	typegroups	
Delete	typeface groups	
Delete and close up	typeface grooups	
Substitute character or part of one or more words	topeface groups	
Wrong fount: replace with correct fount	typeface groups	
Correct damaged characters	typeface groups	
Transpose words	groups typeface	
Transpose characters	ypteface groups	
Transpose lines	the dimension of / is disastrous when	
Transpose lines (2)	the dimension of / is disastrous when	
Centre type	typeface groups	
Indent 1 em	typeface groups	1em
Range left	typeface groups	
Set line or column justified	typeface groups	
Move matter to right	typeface groups	
Move matter to left	typeface groups	
Take down to next line	typeface groups	
Take back to previous line	typeface groups	
Raise matter	typeface groups	
Lower matter	typeface groups	
Correct vertical alignment	typeface groups	
Correct horizontal alignment	typeface groups	
Close up space	t ypeface groups	
Insert space between words	typefacegroups	
Reduce space between words	typeface groups	
Reduce or insert space between letters	ty pe facegroups	
Make space appear equal	typeface groups	
Insert space between lines	aerobic movement. The dimensions of	
Reduce space between paragraphs	aerobic movement. The dimensions of	
Insert parentheses or brackets	typeface groups	
Figure or abbreviation to be spelled out in full	12 point twelve pt	sp.out
Move matter to position indicated	are called the set points dimension	
Set in or change to italics	typeface groups	
Set in or change to capitals	typeface groups	
Set in or change to small capitals	typeface groups	
Capitals for initials, small caps for rest of word	typeface groups	
Set in or change to bold type	typeface groups	
Set in or change to bold italic type	typeface groups	
Change capitals to lower case	typefACE groups	
Change small capitals to lower case	typeface GROUPS	
Change italics to roman	typeface groups	
Invert type	typefaca groups	
Insert ligature	filmsetter	fi
Substitute separate letters for ligature	filmsetter	fi
Insert period	typeface groups	
Insert colon	typeface groups	
Insert semicolon	typeface groups	
Insert comma	typeface groups	
Insert quotation marks	typeface groups	
Insert double quotation marks	typeface groups	
Insert character in superior position	typeface groups	
Substitute character in inferior position	typeface groups	
Insert apostrophe	typeface groups	
Insert ellipsis	typeface groups	
Insert leader dots	typeface groups	
Insert hyphen	typefacegroups	
Insert rule	typeface groups	2pt
Insert oblique	typeface groups	
Start new paragraph	are called points. The questions	
Run on	are called points. The question is	

monti costa Francia

scendere
s
c
e
n
d
e
r
e

gambe di gomma   incontrare una sonagliera un
rosario balzante di suoni al collo d'un galoppo   incontrare un mendicante
= straccio vestito commesso viaggiatore della fame che va sul toboga della via
maestra lungo il mare rotondo sotto il sole biondo coi suoi piedi lunghissimi
100 km.

il **MARE**

quest'altro mendicante azzurro triste   stracci di vele barcacce scarpacce
che fanno acqua   suonare instancabilmente per le vie sotto le finestre

ABOVE: 'The Sea' by Govoni, 1915. An expressive example of 'concrete poetry' that frequently appeared in the Futurist periodical, *Lacerba*.

RIGHT: Many Futurist artists experimented with letter-forms in their 'free-word paintings'. This 'cubist-like' image was produced by Soffici in 1915, entitled 'BIF ZF'.

Futurism and the fine arts

To describe the impact of the various art movements of the early twentieth century as explosive would not be an understatement.

Much of what happened was reactionary. A reaction against the assumption in Art that pictorial reality was unchangeable. Reaction against oppressive government, against unjustice within society, against the accepted ways of doing things, the fear of change. It was a time in history which was ripe for revolution. Its manifestation had many facets. Typographically it came in the form of Futurism.

In stark, total, contrast to the preceding ornate nature of Art Nouveau, Futurism had a form of typographic violence which profoundly affected the future direction of both fine art and graphic design. The movement – which burst out of Italy in 1909 with a vigour not understood at the time – concerned itself with technology and the dynamic aspects of modern life. Its practitioners rejected the classical concepts of harmony and order and strove to express a sense of speed and movement within their work. Their experiments included techniques such as rearranging type from newspapers and magazines to form poems depicting the sounds of modern life.

There is a certain irony that a graphic form, the typeface, was taken by fine artists, cut, distorted, pasted at any angle – long before photo typesetters – without any regard for formal structure, then taken back by graphic designers who then realized the potential and far reaching possibilities of type beyond the basic grid structures of the previous age.

A Futurist practitioner, Filippo Tommaso Marinetti, wrote in the *Lacerba* magazine:

'I am making a typographical revolution which is directed, most of all, against the idiotic, sickening notion of the poetry book with its hand-made papers, its 16th-century style, decorated with galleys, Minervas, Apollos, tall initials, florid ornaments and mythological vegetables with its "motti" and roman numerals. A book must be the futuristic expression of our futuristic thoughts. If necessary, we will use three or four different colours and twenty different type styles on the same page.'

Today, such a quotation may appear overblown but it has to be seen in the context of the period. This was a period before four colour reproduction, before the mass media of magazines and illustrative books. What he was describing was the norm for that period, almost as though there were, or could be, no other way to reproduce the printed word.

Other art movements of the times included Dadaism, Surrealism, and non-representational art. For those people, in this the period of the first world war, the world had gone mad and the only art was non-art and the only sense nonsense. Before a new world could be built the old had to be torn down.

Whilst much of their work might appear playful, meaningless, it had a purpose. It was their way of destroying the values within the arts that had gone before. Typographically they dealt the final blow to the sterility of the medium and reinforced Cubism's concept of the letter as a viable abstract shape, not merely a phonetic form.

But not all modern art of the period was negative. Other movements ran alongside the Anarchists. Movements such as Russian Constructivism, the Bauhaus and the Dutch *De Stijl* all had their influence.

LEFT: 'The Dance of the Serpent' by Severini (1914) used letterforms in an onomatopoetic way to express colours and rhythms.

ABOVE: Marinetti, the rebel of the Futurist movement, produced a major piece of work featuring the 'words-in-freedom' concept, 'Zang Tumb Tuum'. This startling title page and the concrete poem, 'Turkish Captive Balloon' firmly pushed aside classical typographic styling conventions once and for all.

Space, Tone
& Subtleties

5 Space, Tone & Subtleties

The control of space and tone is where graphic designers display their skill and aesthetic judgement.

Variations in line, word and character spacing affect the overall look of body copy. Bold type can look lighter and light type look bolder. The tonal colour – greyness of body copy – will not only be affected by the weight of the typeface, but also by its letterspacing, inter-word spacing and line spacing, and to a lesser extent the line length, although that may affect general readability to a greater extent.

The computer age offers us total control over all forms of spacing. So much so that many agencies and studios develop 'house styles' of spacing for each of their various clients.

Letterspacing

By adjusting inter-character letterspacing it is possible for us to improve legibility in the manner we feel fit for the particular job in hand. This is easily controlled at the computer by the manipulation of each character's designated number of units. By adding to, or subtracting from, the width of set for the various characters, variations in letterspacing can be achieved, either by collective or individual adjustment.

The next section is set in 12/12pt Baskerville with standard letterspacing.

Fashions come and go and this is certainly true of typographical layout and, in particular, letterspacing. The early advantages of computer-generated setting soon made very tight letterspacing fashionable, particularly in headlines. Recently the movement shifted the other way as designers opted for extremely open typography creating a feel reminiscent of the 1950s. As this control over letterspacing allows the tonal colour of body copy to be subtly altered, all designers must remember that at the end of the day they are communicators. Messages have to be read and understood. Too close, or too open, setting done for the sake of fashion at the expense of legibility is NOT good typography.

The passage is repeated but with the set width reduced from standard setting to −1 of standard:

The above style works well and is popular for advertising setting, especially when using serif typefaces. It does not always work so well with condensed sans serif faces because the vertical stress becomes too great, as this short paragraph illustrates. It is set in Univers Light Condensed.

Fashions come and go and this is certainly true of typographical layout and, in particular, letterspacing. The early advantages of computer-generated setting soon made very tight letterspacing fashionable, particularly in headlines. Recently the movement shifted the other way as designers opted for extremely open typography creating a feel reminiscent of the 1950s. As this control over letterspacing allows the tonal colour of body copy to be subtly altered, all designers must remember that at the end of the day they are communicators. Messages have to be read and understood. Too close, or too open, setting done for the sake of fashion at the expense of legibility is NOT good typography.

Fashions come and go and this is certainly true of typographical layout and, in particular, letterspacing. The early advantages of computer-generated setting soon made very tight letterspacing fashionable, particularly in headlines. Recently the movement shifted the other way as designers opted for extremely open typography creating a feel reminiscent of the 1950s. As this control over letterspacing allows the tonal colour of body copy to be subtly altered, all designers must remember that at the end of the day they are communicators. Messages have to be read and understood. Too close, or too open, setting done for the sake of fashion at the expense of legibility is NOT good typography.

RIGHT: When the space reduction in the Baskerville example is overdone legibility is sacrificed. The set width is now reduced to −4.

FAR RIGHT: Extra spacing can work well, but as with minus spacing, it can be overdone. Unpleasant effects are created with +5 spacing.

Fashions come and go and this is certainly true of typographical layout and, in particular, letterspacing. The early advantages of computer-generated setting soon made very tight letterspacing fashionable, particularly in headlines. Recently the movement shifted the other way as designers opted for extremely open typography creating a feel reminiscent of the 1950s. As this control over letterspacing allows the tonal colour of body copy to be subtly altered, all designers must remember that at the end of the day they are communicators. Messages have to be read and understood. Too close, or too open, setting done for the sake of fashion at the expense of legibility is NOT good typography.

Fashions come and go and this is certainly true of typographical layout and, in particular, letterspacing. The early advantages of computer-generated setting soon made very tight letterspacing fashionable, particularly in headlines. Recently the movement shifted the other way as designers opted for extremely open typography creating a feel reminiscent of the 1950s. As this control over letterspacing allows the tonal colour of body copy to be subtly altered, all designers must remember that at the end of the day they are communicators. Messages have to be read and understood. Too close, or too open, setting done for the sake of fashion at the expense of legibility is NOT good typography.

84

In the first example individual characters are kissing, leaving a rather unpleasant style. On the other hand set width can be increased from standard. This next example represents +2 spacing (RIGHT).

This does not read well because of the openness of the character spacing compared to the closeness of the line spacing and is consequently not so easy to read. But when the line feed is increased from 12pt to 16pt a greater degree of legibility is achieved (FAR RIGHT).

Fashions come and go and this is certainly true of typographical layout and, in particular, letterspacing. The early advantages of computer-generated setting soon made very tight letterspacing fashionable, particularly in headlines. Recently the movement shifted the other way as designers opted for extremely open typography creating a feel reminiscent of the 1950s. As this control over letterspacing allows the tonal colour of body copy to be subtly altered, all designers must remember that at the end of the day they are communicators. Messages have to be read and understood. Too close, or too open, setting done for the sake of fashion at the expense of legibility is NOT good typography.

Fashions come and go and this is certainly true of typographical layout and, in particular, letterspacing. The early advantages of computer-generated setting soon made very tight letterspacing fashionable, particularly in headlines. Recently the movement shifted the other way as designers opted for extremely open typography creating a feel reminiscent of the 1950s. As this control over letterspacing allows the tonal colour of body copy to be subtly altered, all designers must remember that at the end of the day they are communicators. Messages have to be read and understood. Too close, or too open, setting done for the sake of fashion at the expense of legibility is NOT good typography.

Fashions come and go and this is certainly true of typographical layout and, in particular, letterspacing. The early advantages of computer-generated setting soon made very tight letterspacing fashionable, particularly in headlines. Recently the movement shifted the other way as designers opted for extremely open typography creating a feel reminiscent of the 1950s. As this control over letterspacing allows the tonal colour of body copy to be subtly altered, all designers must remember that at the end of the day they are communicators. Messages have to be read and understood. Too close, or too open, setting done for the sake of fashion at the expense of legibility is NOT good typography.

Why grapple with the technicalities and jargon of typography . . . . .?
Virtually every piece of visual communication contains typography and designers therefore need to understand how their decisions about spacing, line length and type choice, for instance, increase or hinder the effectiveness of their work.

Wordspacing

Wordspacing can also be controlled, but again too much or too little can affect legibility. The spacing is also affected by the style of typeface chosen. Condensed faces require less space than expanded faces and small type sizes read better with a little extra word spacing. As a general guide, the ideal word space represents one-third to one-half of the width of the lowercase 'o'.

Here are a few examples.

The following text has been set by a 54 unit system with a standard word spacing of 12 units in 10/11pt Univers 55. Too much or too little space between words can seriously affect legibility.

Too little space can cause the individual words to form as one, creating difficulties for the reader in distinguishing one word from another, and too much space can cause rivers which disrupt the natural flow of the eye as it moves from left to right. Rivers are a common problem within narrow justification.

Now with tight word-spacing: 6 units.

Too little space can cause the individual words to form as one, creating difficulties for the reader in distinguishing one word from another, and too much space can cause rivers which disrupt the natural flow of the eye as it moves from left to right. Rivers are a common problem within narrow justification.

This time with very open word spacing: 24 units.

Too little space can cause the individual words to form as one, creating difficulties for the reader in distinguishing one word from another, and too much space can cause rivers which disrupt the natural flow of the eye as it moves from left to right. Rivers are a common problem within narrow justification.

If, with justified setting, word spacing becomes unacceptably wide an increase in the set of the characters can improve the situation. But in general the set should not be increased by more than +3 of the standard width of set so if copy is being typeset at −1, the extra space should ideally not exceed +2 to maintain a good internal balance between characters. Generally speaking these kind of decisions are made by the typesetter but can be modified at proof stage to improve the aesthetic balance of the setting.

Line spacing

Although letter and word spacing are obviously important, the biggest single factor that will affect the tonal grey of the body copy is line spacing. Light type can look strong and medium type weak just by a variation of the line feed. These next examples alter the value of the copy as they progress from −1pt line feed through to +4pt line feed. These examples are set in 9pt Goudy Old Style.

−1pt line feed (9/8pt):

Just as word and letter spacing affect the tonal greys of the body copy, so will the space between each line affect its legibility and tonal colour. The choice of typeface, type size, and line length are other factors to consider, but line spacing decisions are usually made around the correct tonal colour for the design problem rather than being restricted by the norm for the chosen typeface.

Set solid (9/9pt):

Just as word and letter spacing affect the tonal greys of the body copy, so will the space between each line affect its legibility and tonal colour. The choice of typeface, type size, and line length are other factors to consider, but line spacing decisions are usually made around the correct tonal colour for the design problem rather than being restricted by the norm for the chosen typeface.

+1pt line feed (9/10pt):

Just as word and letter spacing affect the tonal greys of the body copy, so will the space between each line affect its legibility and tonal colour. The choice of typeface, type size, and line length are other factors to consider, but line spacing decisions are usually made around the correct tonal colour for the design problem rather than being restricted by the norm for the chosen typeface.

+3pt line feed (9/12pt):

Just as word and letter spacing affect the tonal greys of the body copy, so will the space between each line affect its legibility and tonal colour. The choice of typeface, type size, and line length are other factors to consider, but line spacing decisions are usually made around the correct tonal colour for the design problem rather than being restricted by the norm for the chosen typeface.

+5pt line feed (9/13pt):

Just as word and letter spacing affect the tonal greys of the body copy, so will the space between each line affect its legibility and tonal colour. The choice of typeface, type size, and line length are other factors to consider, but line spacing decisions are usually made around the correct tonal colour for the design problem rather than being restricted by the norm for the chosen typeface.

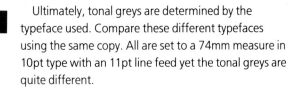

Ultimately, tonal greys are determined by the typeface used. Compare these different typefaces using the same copy. All are set to a 74mm measure in 10pt type with an 11pt line feed yet the tonal greys are quite different.

Excellence in typography is the result of nothing more than an attitude. Its appeal comes from the understanding used in its planning; the designer must care. In contemporary advertising the perfect integration of design elements often demands unorthodox typography. It may require the use of compact spacing, minus leading, unusual sizes and weights; whatever is needed to improve appearance and impact. Stating specific principles or guides on the subject of typography is difficult because the principle applying to one job may not fit the next. No two jobs are identical, even though the text may be.

Excellence in typography is the result of nothing more than an attitude. Its appeal comes from the understanding used in its planning; the designer must care. In contemporary advertising the perfect integration of design elements often demands unorthodox typography. It may require the use of compact spacing, minus leading, unusual sizes and weights; whatever is needed to improve appearance and impact. Stating specific principles or guides on the subject of typography is difficult because the principle applying to one job may not fit the next. No two jobs are identical, even though the text may be.

Excellence in typography is the result of nothing more than an attitude. Its appeal comes from the understanding used in its planning; the designer must care. In contemporary advertising the perfect integration of design elements often demands unorthodox typography. It may require the use of compact spacing, minus leading, unusual sizes and weights; whatever is needed to improve appearance and impact. Stating specific principles or guides on the subject of typography is difficult because the principle applying to one job may not fit the next. No two jobs are identical, even though the text may be.

Subtleties

Once the basics of typography have been absorbed the ambitious designer will look for ways of displaying greater sophistication. The following examples demonstrate some of the minor alterations or additions that can be made to type to give that extra degree of subtlety.

HUNG PUNCTUATION

When body copy is set justified and the punctuation falls at the end of a line the optical effect is a ragged, untidy finish. This can be overcome by increasing the measure of that line by the width of the actual punctuation, and hanging that punctuation outside the line of the column. This may technically create a longer line but optically it has the effect of lining the type up in a straight right hand line. This fine detail is not frequently used when producing a large quantity of body copy as its implementation does mean extra key strokes, slowing down the typesetter and raising the overall cost. However for small quantities it should be used when possible as it improves the final visual effect considerably. (Automatic hung punctuation is now possible with the latest programs.) Hung punctuation can also be used for quotation marks at the beginning of lines which precede the first word.

VISUAL ALIGNMENT

Hanging can be used for letterforms as well as punctuation. It is used in headlines, particularly when they are set in caps. The following headline tells its own story:

When such problems occur they can nowadays be compensated for optically at the keyboard but it may be easier to balance the lines visually, using a scalpel. The letter T is probably the most difficult character to deal with optically. No matter where it is placed it always seems to look wrong. It becomes very much a case of compromise, and may even need a little surgery, reducing the width of the arm of the T. This also applies to other character combinations, LA, for example.

VERTICAL
ALIGNMENT
WILL SEEM
IRREGULAR WHEN
THE FIRST LETTER
OF EACH LINE
DOES NOT BEGIN
WITH A STRAIGHT
VERTICAL STROKE . . .
. . . HOWEVER WHEN LINES
BEGIN WITH THE
LETTERS B, D, E, F,
H, I, K, L, ETC THE
PROBLEM OF ALIGNMENT
DOES NOT OCCUR.

Hyphen, em dash, en dash & parentheses alignment

A small point that is often overlooked is the position of the hyphen, en dash and em dash. They are programmed to centre on the x height as they are mainly used to connect lower case characters or phrases. When set between caps and numerals they are too low. This looks particularly bad in headlines and sub-headings. The correction can be done at the keyboard or with a scalpel.

The same is applicable to the position of parentheses. They are also designed to centre on the x height and require repositioning when used with caps, particularly on headlines.

Line spacing

The importance of inter-character spacing and how it relates to volume not mathematical distance has already been discussed. The same is true of inter-line spacing on headlines.

Without linefeed adjustment

consecutive lines without descenders
or ascenders may appear
further away from those lines with
only a few or none at all.

With linefeed adjustment

consecutive lines without descenders
or ascenders may appear
further away from those lines with
only a few or none at all.

To compensate for the optical defects the typesetter will need an accurate trace to follow. In such circumstances, it may be simpler to specify the line feed in millimetres rather than points, if the headline is in a big size. The modern computer can cope with mixed measurements.

Ligatures

A ligature is a special character joining two or more characters. They occur in serif faces and the most common are fi, fl, ff, ffi and ffl. They are a throwback from the days of hot metal setting when they were created to deal with the problem of overhanging part of the letter f. Consequently some modern fonts do not carry a full set of ligatures. That's a pity because they are an added refinement to typographic design. They have a drawback if letterspacing is not standard. The ligature is of a fixed character space and therefore, if the text is set very tight or very open the ligature could look odd.

first flush flat fling efficient
Without ligatures

first flush flat fling efficient
With ligatures

first flush flat fling efficient
Tight setting without ligatures

first flush flat fling efficient
Tight setting with ligatures

first flush flat fling efficient
Open setting without ligatures

first flush flat fling efficient
Open setting with ligatures

The above are the common ligatures but others can be developed by the designer, particularly in headline setting. Diphthongs can also be ligatured, when the vowels a and e, and e and o are sounded as one, such as in the word Caesar. They look like this: Æ, æ, Œ, œ.

Small caps

Small caps, indicated as 'sc', are capital letters which
have been redrawn to match the weight of the lower
case x height. They are extremely useful when used in
conjunction with the standard typesize, as a substitute
for caps in abbreviations where the use of full size caps
can become over-assertive and dominant. They are
particularly useful in stationery design for listing
qualifications.

Unfortunately most typesetting systems do not carry
small caps as standard – true small caps should be
special fonts designed to match the actual typeface.
Consequently there is a limited choice in small caps
fonts. Technically it is possible to set full size caps at the
size of the x height in any face but there is a subtle
difference in weight, as the examples below illustrate.

12pt Bembo Roman set with
TRUE SMALL CAPS

12pt Bembo Roman set with
SMALL CAPS set by reduction

Notice how the stem of the small caps character
balances with the stem of the lower case character in
the TRUE SMALL CAPS example, whereas the stem of the
SMALL CAP is lighter than that of the lower case character
in the electronically reduced example. The use of caps
and small caps is also quite popular for use in headlines
and packaging, and provides a welcome contrast from
some other styles.

Emphasis

Almost every job will require some form of emphasis in
its design – headlines, sub-headings, the use of colour.
Sometimes emphasis is required within the actual body
copy and there are various ways in which this can be
achieved. The style chosen will most likely depend upon
the degree of emphasis required.

When deciding which words or phrases require
emphasis, and to what degree, remember that too
much emphasis can have the opposite effect. Overlong
phrases can lose their impact if the reader loses track of
where extra stress was intended. The amount of copy,
and where it occurs within the main body, will affect
how the emphasis is treated. The single word in the
middle of a large section of body copy can easily be
lost with the wrong treatment, and will possibly need a
different emphasis than if it occurred at the beginning
of a paragraph.

The use of italic is a simple method of *drawing
attention* to the single word or short phrase. It is a
simple method of highlighting the occasional word or
phrase *without altering the tonal colour of the copy.*

If the copy requires greater emphasis it can be
achieved by the introduction of capital letters to PROVE
A POINT, but their inclusion would cause the balance
and readability to suffer IF THE PHRASE WENT ON AND
ON FOR FAR TOO LONG.

On the other hand the introduction of small caps can
offer a different ALTERNATIVE to the more aggressive
FULL SIZE capital. Tonally, they carry the same emphasis
as the use of the italic, but have a slightly more formal
edge.

Probably the most common method of increasing
emphasis is by the introduction of a heavier weight of
the same typeface, light to medium, medium to bold.
It attracts attention and is hard to ignore. Unlike italics,
caps and small caps, **it will have a greater effect
upon the tonal balance of the layout.** That should
be the very reason for using type in a heavier weight of
type, as an attention-getter.

The introduction of a different typeface within the
body copy needs far greater control and consequently
is rarely used. The reasons for change have to be
sound. Other than in sub-headings, titles or captions it
is rarely effective. However, in magazine and illustrative
book production, different type is used but is normally
separated from the main body copy by the use of space
and rules.

If different fonts are mixed within the same text,
faces with contrasting styles are necessary, so that it
looks deliberate. In this case look for opposites. A sans
serif alongside a serif will obviously give contrast but
Univers mixed with Helvetica or Bodoni with Modern
No 20 will suggest that a mistake has been made.

91

When mixing fonts remember that the same point size caps and x heights will vary from face to face and that size adjustment to one of the faces may be required to produce a matching cap or x height. This is also true of some faces when they change from roman to italic. Perpetua Roman, for example, has a larger x height than its equivalent size in italic.

The above methods of creating emphasis need to be handled with both taste and care. Creating emphasis is obviously an integral feature of design but if the various styles are mishandled, with over-emphasis, or too much mixing of styles, the effect will be lost and general legibility be reduced.

Underscoring

This is another form of emphasis and can be used within general body setting. Normally the underscore falls just below the base line and should break for descenders. It can be aligned below the descenders as well, so as not to cause a break. The typesetter can adjust their thickness but normally they look best when they match the width of the horizontal lines in the chosen typeface.

A more common use of the underscore occurs within advertising headlines. Whilst an underscore can be typeset, it often requires additional retouching at the larger point sizes to produce the best optical result. When typeset the ends of the underscore finish square which is where the optical defects occur, particularly when the setting is in italic. The square corners look strange against the round edges of descenders, particularly on g and y. When such refinement is required it could be simpler for an artist to follow a master trace and draw an entire underscore by hand.

Display initials

An introductory initial to a section of text can be raised, dropped and hung. The raised initial aligns on the base line of the first line of text.

A raised initial can be varied further by an indent. If the required typeface cannot be included on the machine with the main body copy, the typesetter should be asked to indent the first line the required amount of space so that the initial can be stripped in by hand later.

Dropped initials require a set number of lines to be indented, leaving space for the initial to be set on one of the lower base lines. The number of lines the initial cap takes up is at the discretion of the designer but the top of the cap should align with the top of the cap height of the first line of text.

Hung initials are the least common of the three. They normall hang outside the left hand margin and are dropped to align with one of the lower base lines and the top of the cap height on the first line.

There are variations and combinations of the above. For example, a hung initial can be hung whilst aligning with the first base line giving the effect of being both hung and raised.

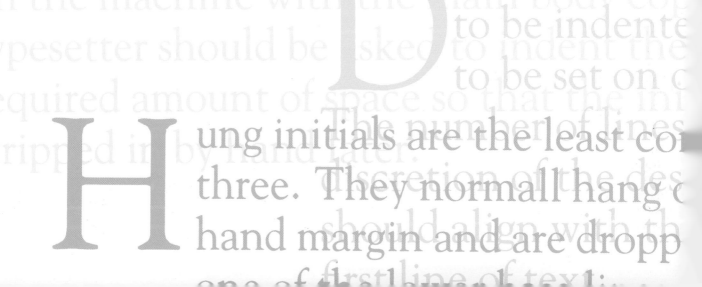

Another variation for the hung character is for it to be half raised, half dropped. Unless using the latest computers this will have to be positioned by hand to make sure that the base alignment is correct. Nothing looks worse, and this applies to all typography, than a non-aligning base line.

When a dropped initial has an awkward shape, such as the W in this paragraph, the type should follow the contour of its shape rather than be set as a vertically positioned indent.

Indeed all three styles can be combined: half hung, half raised, half dropped, but the typeface and character must be chosen with care. A capital L would be difficult to use within these particular variations. The success of all of the different styles is very much dependent upon the actual character and chosen typeface. Whatever you decide it is always a good idea to send your typesetter a layout of what you have in mind.

Ranged body copy

In the chapter on copyfitting the possibilities of the ranged left and ranged right style and their advantages of even word spacing were discussed. The disadvantage of the style is if the copy is accepted as it comes, direct from the machine, without any aesthetics being applied to its visual presentation. Ideally ragged setting style requires short and long lines to alternate. This is demonstrated in the next paragraph.

Whilst the option of whether to hyphenate or not to hyphenate is a personal decision, for some reason the great majority of ranged copy seems to be without hyphenation. The result of this is often a succession of ugly line endings, some to the full measure, others very short leaving large holes. With careful editing this can be overcome by altering the line endings and by the intelligent use of hyphenation. Ideally what we require are alternate lines of short, long, short, long.

Whilst the option of whether to hyphenate or not to hyphenate is a personal decision, for some reason the great majority of ranged copy seems to be without hyphenation. The result of this is often a succession of ugly line endings, some to the full measure, others very short leaving large holes. With careful editing this can be overcome by altering the line endings and by the intelligent use of hyphenation. Ideally what we require are alternate lines of short, long, short, long.

Numerals

Designers often choose whatever numerals come with the rest of the text face, which does not have to be the case. There are some beautiful numeral designs and greater awareness of their existence would be helpful. Numerals can be separated into two distinct categories – Old Style and Modern. The Old Style numerals are also called non-lining, and have the same characteristics as the lower case alphabet, with ascenders and descenders. Modern numerals follow the style of the capital letter, being all the same cap height. They are also called 'lining' or 'ranging' numerals.

Old Style numerals are most suited to general body copy where numerals do not have any special emphasis, since they match lower case characters. On the other hand Modern numerals are good for emphasis as they stand out strongly by aligning with the cap height. They are also called 'non-lining' numerals.

Unfortunately most numerals today are now Modern, which can be restrictive for some specific jobs. If a commission features numerals strongly it would be advisable to choose your typeface because of its style of numerals. If your typesetter has a restricted range of fonts and not the Old Style numerals of your choice a compromise might be to set the Modern numerals in a smaller point size to reduce their dominance.

93

Ranging numerals

1 2 3 4 5
6 7 8 9 0

Old Style numerals

1 2 3 4 5
6 7 8 9 0

Ampersand

The ampersand, an abbreviation for the word 'and', is one of the most beautiful shapes in typography. It should be taken full advantage of wherever and whenever possible. Whilst it is not suitable for use in body copy it has tremendous possibilities in headlines, and particularly in packaging and display.

Punctuation

Punctuation can be easily overlooked or taken for granted. The hanging of punctuation to preserve the straight vertical edge of setting has already been discussed and there are other areas where the modification of punctuation can improve the aesthetic quality of a design.

In abbreviations the typesetter normally leaves a word space following each punctuation mark but this is not always necessary. For example the standard word spacing between the punctuation of

Mr. L. Y. Harris,

as here, is far too great. Depending upon the character combinations this could easily be reduced to half word spacing or in the case of the combination L. Y. to zero wordspacing.

Mr. L. Y. Harris, York House, 45 Vernon Road, West Midlands.

normal word spacing

Mr. L.Y. Harris, York House, 45 Vernon Road, West Midlands.

tight wordspacing after abbreviations

Whilst modifications can cause additional machine time they are worth the effort, particularly in larger sizes of type and in company stationery.

There are also circumstances when punctuation marks should be set smaller. Their appearance in bold display headlines can often be over assertive if there happens to be an unusual number.

"Full stops, com

same size punctuation

"Full stops, com

reduced size punctuation

The above clearly demonstrates the superior balance when the punctuation is reduced by only a single point. On the other hand, greater emphasis can be gained by increasing the size of punctuation marks. In those circumstances the punctuation becomes a design feature rather than a requirement of language. When the scale of the punctuation is considerably increased it is always wise to provide the typesetter with an accurate trace of exactly what is required.

95

When the scale of the punctuation is considerably increased it is always wise to provide the typesetter with an accurate trace of exactly what is required.

Em dash and en dash

All type fonts should carry both an em dash and an en dash. Their design is both thinner and longer than the hyphen and their use is different from that of the hyphen. They have distinct uses, principally to separate phrases, and not to join or separate individual words as is the case with the hyphen. As their name implies they are based upon the width of the en and em space. The en dash has two particular functions. It is used instead of parentheses, to create a break in a sentence, and it is used as a substitute for the word 'to', as in dates or phrases like 'the London—Brighton train'. Some designers specify the em dash for those two functions but it tends to be too long and looks inelegant. When the en dash is used parenthetically it should have a word space on each side.

Dingbats, boxes and bullets

There are many ways in which basic copy can be given extra life, interest and vitality. The only restriction is the designer's aesthetic judgement and good taste, and they should know when to stop.

The most decorative form of embellishment comes in the form of the dingbat (or colophon). There is a range of these available covering all manner of shapes and styles and these can be introduced into copy as taste and function dictate. They can be ordered from a typesetter in the same way as the rest of your type by specifying their overall depth, or to match x or cap height.

If the dingbat is too decorative for a particular purpose a simpler alternative is the box or bullet. Both are available in solid or open form and have a variety of uses. The open box is ideal for integration into forms and coupons for customer response or a checklist but can also serve as a decoration for the conclusion of chapters, paragraphs or captions.

Most pi fonts (typesetters' special fonts, which include characters not normally found on standard type fonts, such as symbols, mathematical signs, reference signs etc) carry three sizes of box or bullet for setting on line (simultaneously) to match x, cap and body height. To match a box or bullet with a particular x or cap height it might be necessary to specify a different point size. A bullet to be set at x height between caps will need to be raised to centre between the caps otherwise it will look wrong.

☛ LETTERS alone are not always enough ⁎⁎ when something a little different is required try • ● ⬤ bullets, ▪ ■ ■ boxes or ★ ♦ △ dingbats. ¶ They can add *visual spice* to mundane subjects, they can help to justify lines ▷ ▷ ▷ ▷ ▷ ▷ ▷ ▷ ▷ ▷ ▷ ▷ or simply point the reader in the right direction ☞

bauhaus

and sans serif type

abcdefghi
jklmnopqr
stuvwxyz

By far the most important and influential graphic design movement prior to the second world war began in Germany in 1919. The architect, Walter Gropius, was invited by the Grand Duke of Weimar to integrate the local art academy with the arts and crafts school. The new institute was called 'Das Staatliche Bauhaus Weimar', or more simply, the 'Bauhaus'. Gropius set out to recruit the finest, most creative minds of the day: Paul Klee, Wassily Kandinsky and Lionel Feininger amongst them, plus a visiting faculty drawn from some of the leading avant-garde movements of the day. Their theories created numerous innovative designs covering books, posters, catalogues, exhibitions, typefaces and a publication called *Bauhausbücher*.

Because of the unstable political situation throughout Germany, the school was forced to move several times throughout the 1920s and was finally forced to close in 1933. It was perceived as a threat by the Nazi Party. Following the closure its students dispersed all over Europe and America, taking with them the Bauhaus philosophy.

Although the Bauhaus was only in existence for fourteen years its teachings had a major impact upon twentieth-century design. Whilst its style is only occasionally mimicked today, a great deal of our current graphic design can be traced back to Bauhaus influences and teachings. It set out to bring together art and industry, believing that the machine was just as capable of producing objects of beauty as those made by hand. In order to achieve this, students had to have both technical and theoretical training. The basics of design and layout were combined with a knowledge of how to exploit the latest innovations in photography, typesetting and printing. This may be standard in art schools today but it was revolutionary at that time.

TOP LEFT: The design of the title of the Bauhaus journal from 1929 onwards, when Joost Schmidt took over the design. His alteration was to remove the last serifs on the a and to reverse out the whole title.

MIDDLE LEFT: Universal type designed by Herbert Bayer in 1925.

LEFT: This collage by Lou Scheper was a tribute to the artist Florence Henri. It was also a means of experimenting with different kinds of type, for which collage became very popular.

BELOW: The label for this typewriter ribbon tin was designed in 1924–5 by Joost Schmidt, who taught at the Bauhaus from 1925. Russian Constructivism had a big influence on Bauhaus thinking, and that influence can be seen here.

The Bauhaus was not specifically a graphic design school but as the school developed, graphics, and in particular, typography, played a very important role as their production of posters and publications increased. The Hungarian Laszlo Moholy-Nagy was one of the first members to promote typography at the school when he became involved with the production of the various publications. His statement 'Typography must be clear communication in the most vivid form . . . clarity is the essence of modern printing' says much about Bauhaus layout with its style of simple, asymmetrical layouts and balance, a dominance of sans serif faces, a feel for white space as never before witnessed and the creative use of geometric rectangles and circles, not as ornaments, but as functional guidelines to take the eye through the message.

This dominant use of sans serif faces for body copy was both new and revolutionary. The terms 'Grotesque' and 'Gothic' that appeared in the early nineteenth century to describe the new sans serif designs were used sparingly and specifically for display and advertising purposes. This was the first time that the sans serif had dominated so strongly.

LEFT: This catalogue cover was designed by El Lissitsky for the first exhibition of avant-garde Russian art to be held outside Russia. It was held at the Galerie Van Dieman in Berlin in 1922.

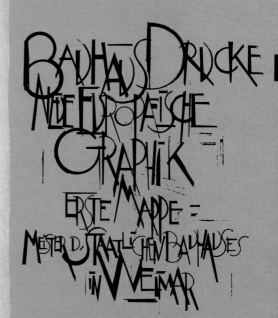

ABOVE: The title page of the portfolio *New European Style (Neue Europaeische Graphik)*, 1921. Designed by Lyonel Feininger, the typography gives an exuberant and personal touch to what might otherwise be a solemn-looking page.

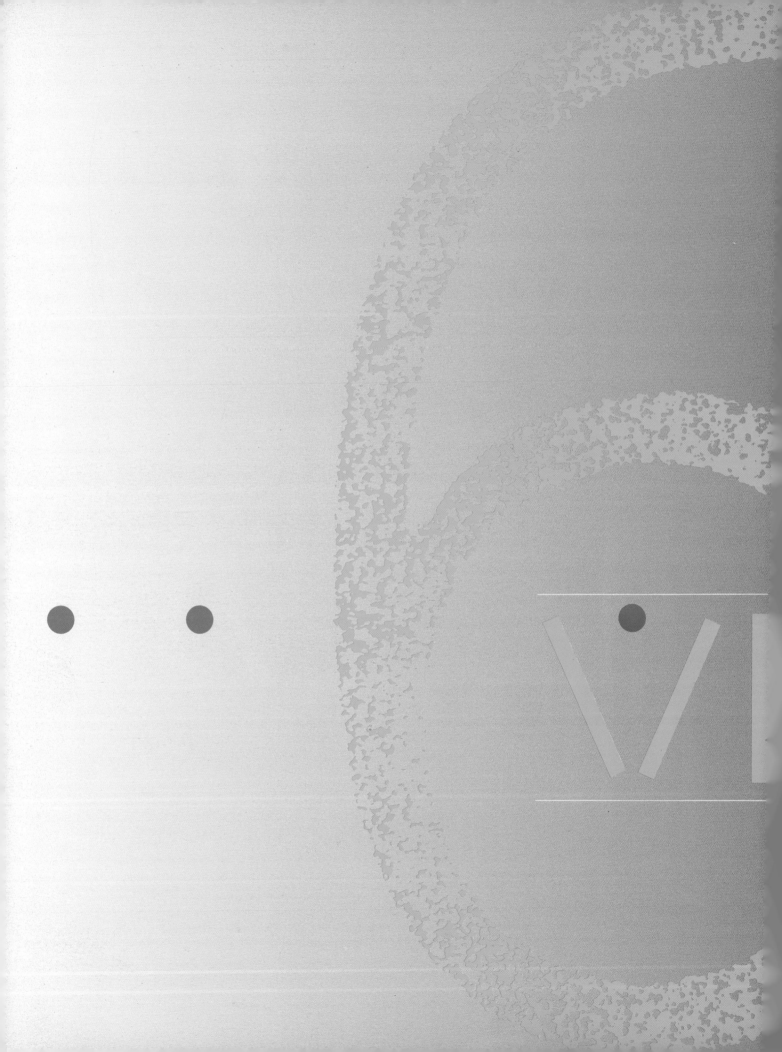

Photography
and the
Computer Age

6 Photography and the Computer Age

Modern technology provides all graphic designers with numerous opportunities to enhance and develop their work. This is particularly so for the creative typographer.

Virtually every edition of any computer magazine offers newer and more advanced programs for the designer. It may not be too long before all of the more traditional methods of photographic manipulation of type will be replaced by the computer. Most are available now but only a few of these are generally affordable.

The distortion of type using camera lenses has been available for many years. Italicized, condensed and expanded type are all simple to achieve. Other machines can add any multiple combination of inline, outline, or dropped shadow. Some can set type in circles, or in wavy lines, in balls, with perspective distortion and so on.

A simple description of the phototypesetter would be to call it a rather complex photographic enlarger. Each typographic character is held on a film negative or glass screen and then exposed, at speed, onto a photographic material. Whilst such systems are very slow by modern standards, they give a better quality of image; but even this is changing as computer systems make further progress.

RIGHT: This character was set on a CRT (cathode ray tube) typesetter. These work in either of two ways. In the first, data is stored in the computer and the type generated electronically from a digital fount on to the video tube. From there, it is transferred to photo-sensitive paper or film. In the second, a photographic fount is scanned by the machine to recreate the characters. In both, the characters are made up of dots or lines.

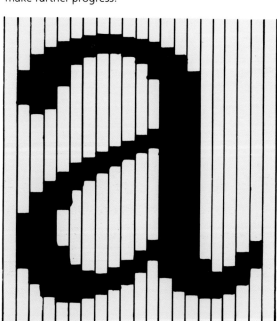

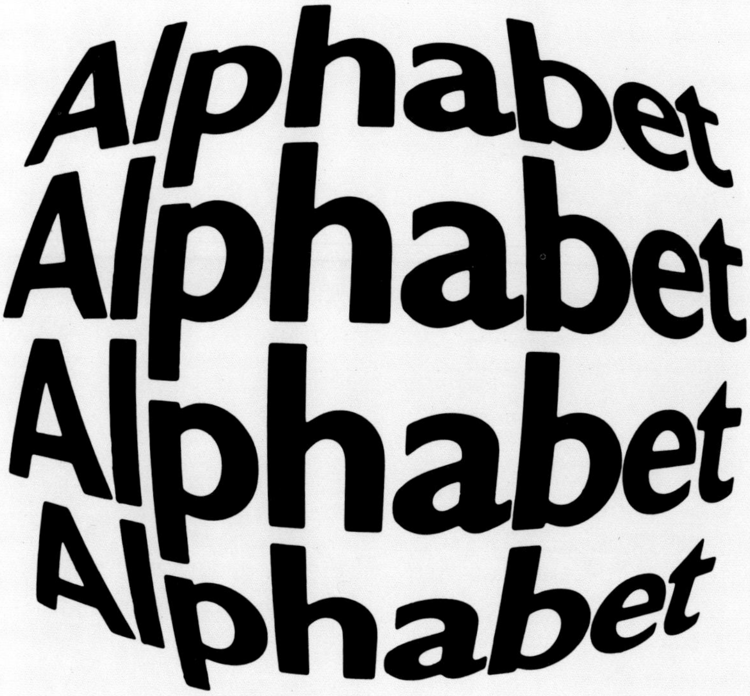

Alphabet
Alphabet
Alphabet
Alphabet

ALPHABET
PERSPECTIVE

ALPHABET
PERSPECTIVE

Effects created by typesetters. Modern computerised equipment enables type suppliers to produce all kinds of effects, and many type houses show stock effects in their catalogues. There is no need, though, to limit yourself to these, most typesetters can reproduce virtually any effect you specify.

ALPHABET
PERSPECTIVE

Trick Face
Trick Face
Trick Face
Trick Face
Trick Face
Trick Face
Trick Face
Trick Face
Trick Face
Trick Face
Trick Face
Trick Face

Modification
Modification
Modification
Modification

104

Distortion can be used to
emphasise meaning, as
these examples
demonstrate. In addition,
numerous enhancements
can provide endless variety
to a single phrase (see
'Trick Face' examples).

After the phototypesetter, the next generation of typesetters were totally computer-based. Images were produced via a cathode ray tube (CRT). Each typographic character was digitized into a grid of small pixels, often more than 1000 per 25mm. Each pixel was exposed onto photographic material to make up the typographic character. The latest typesetters are similar in principle to the earlier CRT machines but instead of using a cathode ray tube to produce the image, this is constructed by a laser beam. This means that they are faster and their quality is superior especially as the type size increases.

Personal computers linked to laser printers now make it possible for graphic designers to work with type on screen and print out the results all at one desk, hence the term 'desktop publishing' (DTP). There are a variety of DTP systems, some more sophisticated and having more facilities than others. There are simple systems, used primarily to improve the presentation of business reports and statistics, while the sophisticated graphics programs available allow the designer to try out almost any possibility and see the results instantly. Rapid development of these systems has meant that many designers are now using DTP systems within their studios.

BELOW: The use of computers in design presents new opportunities to typographers. In addition to inputting the type specification directly into the computers themselves, they can create and view their layouts very quickly. Specifications and layouts can also be amended easily.

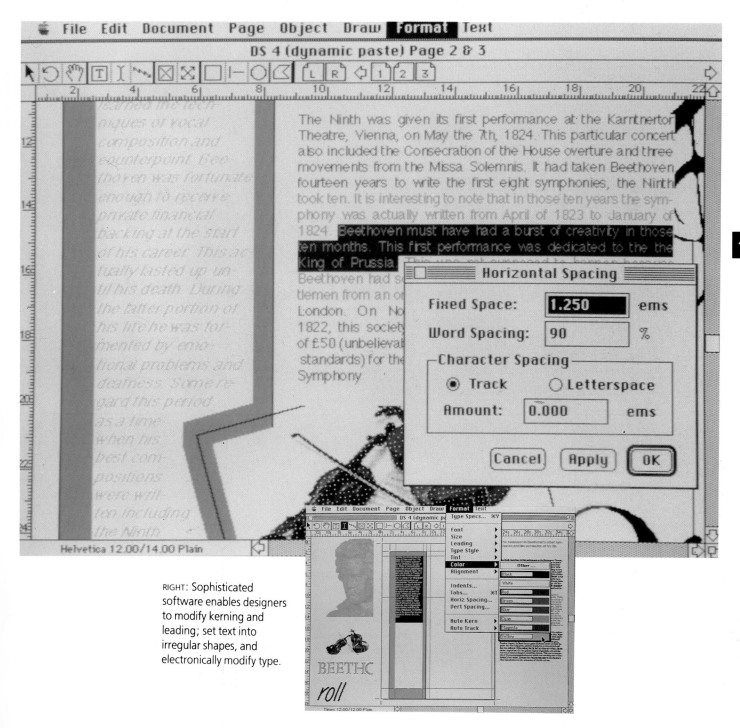

RIGHT: Sophisticated software enables designers to modify kerning and leading; set text into irregular shapes, and electronically modify type.

Many graphic
designers now use a
computer workstation in
preference to a drawing
board.

There are many advantages of working with DTP systems, both for designers and their clients. Word-processed text can be transferred into a graphics program and dropped into a grid already created and stored on the computer. Rules and pictures keylines can be created and positioned, and the whole page viewed on screen. (This is known as 'wysiwyg' – 'what you see is what you get'.) Fonts can be chosen, enlarged, reduced, changed and manipulated easily and quickly to suit any design. Images can be drawn and painted on screen, or, using a scanner, existing images can be 'scanned' into the system. Images can also be manipulated, changed and coloured, and incorporated into a design. Working with type in a 'draw' program and combining the results with a graphics program gives greater flexibility to the designer. Editing text and other typographical changes can easily be made without incurring the delay and cost of conventional typesetting. After all work on text and visuals is complete, the design can be output at artwork quality ready for printing.

DTP is an excellent design tool, but designers should never allow their creativity to be constrained by the limitations of computers. Computers *cannot* make aesthetic judgements; the designer must always control the computer, harnessing the power and flexibility of new technology to enhance those typographic design details and so often make or break the design of visual communication material.

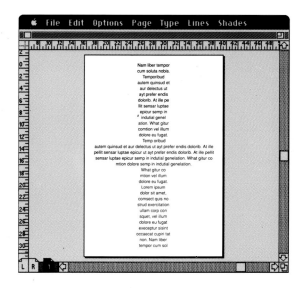

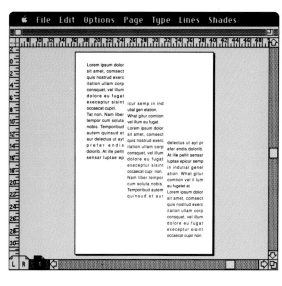

LEFT: DTP software allows the typographic designers to create numerous text shapes with relative ease. All these examples can be produced directly by the designer using a few keystrokes. Using conventional methods of layout and typesetting these shapes would take many hours to create.

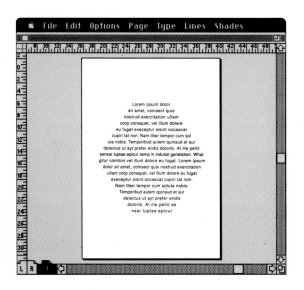

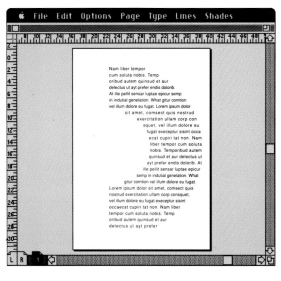

RIGHT: Some publications –
particularly magazines and
newsletters – are
particularly suited to design
using computers. Once the
text and typographic
specification has been
keyed-in, and a page grid
created, alternative layouts
can easily be designed. The
main advantage of using
computers in this way is
that the designer can easily
and quickly see a facsimile
of his or her work.

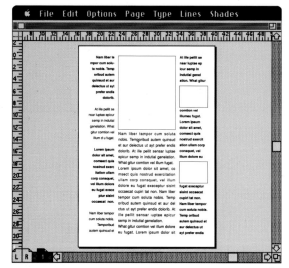
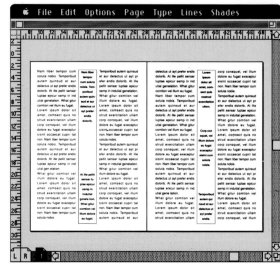

108

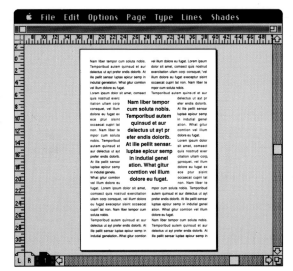
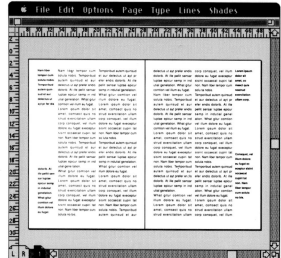

RIGHT: Greater impact has
been achieved by using the
article headings in a very
graphic way. The headlines
in these two examples have
been manipulated by using
the computer and
incorporated with the text
into a double page layout.

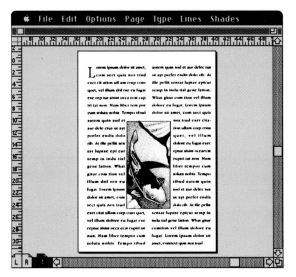

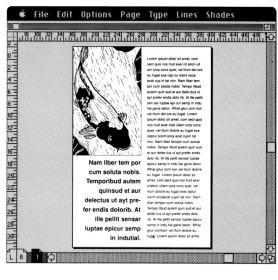

LEFT: Many DTP systems allow for the 'scanning' or 'grabbing' of photographs and illustrations. These can be cropped, retouched and electronically modified to enhance their impact. Images can be 'merged' with type into the grid and the layout designed on screen.

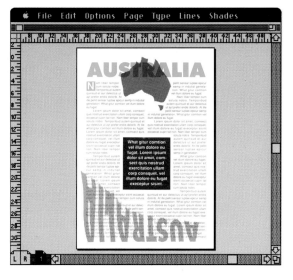

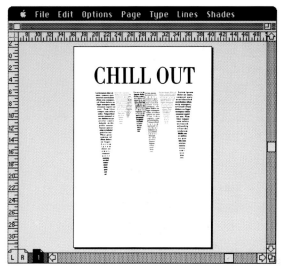

LEFT: Most computer page make-up systems incorporate the three printer's base colours of cyan blue, magenta and red, in addition to black. Designing with a colour monitor, these colours can be displayed on screen. Colours can be mixed together to add life and impact to the typographic designs.

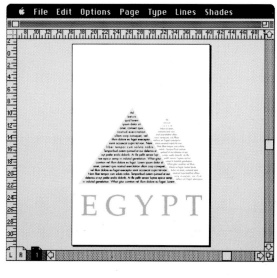

Neville Brody — the rule breaker

It is always difficult to know how to evaluate the importance of an artist of our era, to assess how his or her work will stand the test of time. Whatever the answer to these questions may prove to be, the work of one British designer, Neville Brody, is certainly different. He has taken chances and is not afraid to stand every typographic rule upon its head.

Born in North London, he started his design career in 1975 at the Hornsey College of Art on a Fine Art foundation course. In spite of his own fine art tendencies he could not see a way forward in his pursuit of what to him seemed to be an 'élitist form' which only appealed to the gallery market. He wanted to create something broader, something with which his generation could identify.

So he entered graphic design on a three-year BA course at the London School of Printing. This is a college with a strong reputation for the finer points of typography, with a staple diet of historical figures like Baskerville, Gill and Morison. However he found this strong craft bias to be repressive and stultifying. And his tutors condemned his work as 'uncommercial', preferring the safer commercial strategies to his natural tendencies towards experimentation.

In the late 1970s, when Punk Rock was having a major effect upon young Londoners, Brody was no exception. The anarchic dress, attitudes and music of the punks were just the catalyst he needed. To quote Brody from his book, *The Graphic Language of Neville Brody,* where he said, 'My design went in for servicing and came out supercharged. I'd gone to the LCP because it had the reputation for being the hardest graphic design course in Europe, not hard as in difficult, but pure. I felt that if you wanted to react against anything you had to learn about that thing totally. Punk hit me fast, and it gave me the confidence I needed. I believe that you should pursue an idea, do it, stop, then go on to the next one.'

Brody was continually at odds with his tutors, an important factor in how his own, very personal, style emerged. That factor was the catalyst he needed to pursue his own totally independent and unique way of handling layout and, in particular, type. Without that antagonism, tension and conflict, would he have had that same self-determination to be different? His comment, that if you want to break the rules you must first understand what they are, is very pertinent to his work. Whilst his work may break every rule in the book, his designs all contain the basic fundamentals necessary for successful design. Internal balance, space and proportion are evident in all of what he has produced.

FAR LEFT: Logo for Post, furnishing design partnership.

ABOVE: Continuity within magazine design is important. This W had appeared in the previous edition of *The Face* in an inverted form to highlight an article on the singer, Madonna.

LEFT: The logo for 'Expo' which appeared in the February 85 edition of *The Face* magazine.

ABOVE TOP: The death of Typography! or is it the birth of a new way of typographic thinking?

ABOVE: This logo of the word 'style' for *The Face* was taken through several transitions of abstraction.

LEFT: The bold version of the geometric 'Typeface Six' designed for *The Face* magazine to replace the existing Futura.

A B C D E F G H I I
J K L M N O P Q R !
S T U V W X Y Z [?]

bcdefghijklmnop
rstuvwxyzéè!?()

ABOVE: This typeface was developed from Brody's design of the word 'avanti', a main heading for one of the pages of the magazine *Arena*. Available only in the lowercase form, Brody has since applied the face to other sections of the magazine.

BELOW: Logo for the magazine distributors, Comag.

In his first year thesis Brody drew a comparison between the Dadaists and Pop Art. The 'anti-art' of Dada, the strong colour of Pop Art, Futurism's disregard for typographic convention and the Bauhaus desire for construction and awareness of the latest technologies were all absorbed into his work.

His greatest appeal is probably his rather 'quirky' typeface and logo designs. Some have a strong 1930s feel, others are almost abstract, but above all they all have life, imagination, and most importantly are a creative reflection of the period's times and attitudes. He has put a new life and vitality into British and international typography.

LEFT: 'This is SOCA 2'. A highly colourful design for a record sleeve featuring distinctively strong, hand-drawn type.

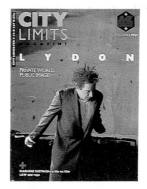

Three cover designs. ABOVE: *The Face*. This cover (March 1985) typifies the conviction of *The Face*'s tag-line, 'The World's Best Dressed Magazine'.

LEFT: Another important area of Brody's work concerned the magazine, *City Limits*. When he joined the magazine in 1983 his first task was to redesign the basic grid structure of the magazine.

LEFT: *Arena* appeared in 1986 and was seen as a magazine for readers who had grown out of *The Face*, and also a publication for men. There were no men's magazines of its type in England at the time.

V II

7

Faults to Avoid

7 Faults to Avoid

The following section is a checklist of problems that might occur in typography, which the designer should attempt to rectify before the job is completed.

Widows

A common weakness in text setting is the widow, where the final word of a paragraph is given a whole line of its own. A long word set to a short measure does not matter too much but if the measure is wide, more than 40 characters per line or so imbalance is created within the tonality of the design.

The problem can usually be quite easily rectified by one of three methods:

1. Check back through the text for the possibilities of hyphenation. A broken word earlier on can quite easily lose the widow when the text is re-run.

2. If the introduction of a hyphen is not possible, take a short word or syllable from one line ending over to the next line and re-run the remainder of the text. The re-run may cause the final line to be extended by another word or two.

3. Work with the copywriter to see if some of the copy can be reworded, either to include or omit a word or two.

Orphans

The orphan is the single word paragraph end taken over from the foot of one column to the head of the next column or page. This is also the term for a final line taken over to the next column. All of these can be avoided by similar methods as for widows.

Rivers

Rivers occur when consecutive word spaces – often excessively word spaced – appear below each other causing vertical areas of white space. They normally occur within short measures of justified type and can be difficult to rectify. An increase in the inter character spacing of some of the lines will help to reduce excessive word spacing. A more satisfactory answer would be to alter the style of justification to a ranged style.

Length of measure

An over-long measure can spoil readability and understanding. The ideal number of characters per line for body copy is between 36 and 50. When the number of characters goes well beyond that, ie 80 or more, readability suffers considerably as a re-run of this paragraph demonstrates.

Length of measure

An over-long measure can spoil readability and understanding. The ideal number of characters per line for body copy is between 36 and 50. When the number of characters goes well beyond that, ie 80 or more, readability suffers considerably as a re-run of this paragraph demonstrates.

Lorem ipsum dolor sit amet, consectetur adipiscing elit, sed diam zum nonnumy eiusmodn empor incidunt ut labore et dolore magna aliqua erar volupat. Ut enim adminim veniam, quis nostrud exercitation nisi ut aliquip ex ea commodo consequat. Duis autem vel eum irure dolor in reprehenderit in volupante velit esse moledtaie consequat, vel illum dolore eu.

Lorem ipsum dolor sit amet, consectetur adipiscing elit, sed diam zum nonnumy eiusmodn empor incidunt ut labore et dolore magna aliqua erar volupat. Ut enim adminim veniam, quis nostrud exercitation nisi ut aliquip ex ea commodo consequat. Duis autem vel eum irure dolor in reprehenderit in volupante velit esse moledtaie consequat, vel illum dolore eu ugiat nulla pariatur. At vero eos et accusam et iusto odiom dignissim qui blandit praesent lutatum delenit aigue duos dolor et se molestias exceptuer sint occaesat cupidat non provident, simil sunt it culpa qui officia deserunt millit anim id est laborum et dolor fuga. Lorem ipsum dolor sit amet, consectetur adipiscing elit, sed diam zum nonnumy eiusmodn empor

incidunt ut labore.

Et dolore magna aliqua erar volupat. Ut enim adminim veniam, quis nostrud exercitation nisi ut aliquip ex ea commodo consequat. Duis autem vel eum irure dolor in reprehenderit in volupante velit esse moledtaie consequat, vel illum dolore eu fugiat nulla pariatur. At vero eos et accusam et iusto odiom dignissim qui blandit praesent lutatum delenit aigue duos dolor et se molestias exceptuer sint occaesat cupidat non provident, simil sunt it culpa qui officia deserunt millit anim id est laborum et dolor fuga. Et harumd dereud facilis est er expedit distinct. Nam liber tempor cumet soluta nobis eligend optio comgue hinil impedit doming in quodmaxit placeat

Lorem ipsum dolor sit amet, consectetur adiscing elit, sed diam zum nonnumy eiusmodn empor incidunt ut labore et dolore magna erar volupat. Ut enim adminim veniam, quis nostrud exercitation aliquip ex commodo consequat. Duis autem eum irure dolor in reprehenderit in volupante velit moledtaie consequat, dolore eu ugiat nulla pariatur. At vero eos et accusam et iusto odiom dignissim qui blandit lutatum delenit aigue dolor et se molestias exceptuer sint occaesat cupidat non provident, simil it culpa qui deserunt millit id est laborum et fuga. Lorem ipsum dolor sit amet, consectetur

adipiscing elit, sed.

Diam zum nonnumy eiusmodn empor incidunt ut labore et magna erar volupat. Ut enim adminim veniam, quis nostrud nisi ut aliquip ex ea commodo consequat. Duis autem vel eum reprehenderit in volupante velit esse moledtaie consequat, dolore eu fugiat pariatur. At veroeos accusam et odiom dignissim qui blandit praesent delenit aigue duos et molestias sint occaesat cupidat non provident, simil it culpa qui deserunt millit anim est dolor fuga. Et harumd facilis est er expedit distinct. Nam

Legibility of body copy

Body text does not always have to be printed in black but there is a reason for the predominance of black on white. Readability tests have proved that black type on white paper has the best readability characteristics, with the greater the volume of copy the greater that readability. If full colour is being used in the job then for small sizes of type (below 14pt) the only colours available to the designer will be the three primary colours: cyan, magenta and yellow, printed as flat colour. Other colours are possible with a fifth printing impression and extra cost.

For larger sizes – dependent upon typeface suitability – type can be printed in a wide variety of colours mixed from the primaries, but this rarely happens in advertising copy. The reason is one of readability.

White type reversed out of black is visually strong, but if the wrong face is used readability is seriously affected. A fine serif below 14pt for large areas of text is not good practice because the text is not very legible. The quality of platemaking and particularly the inking of the press rollers has got to be as near perfect as possible as there is a strong tendency for the serifs to fill in, and if the typeface contains fine hairline strokes these can also be lost.

Type can be reversed out of a four-colour combination, as opposed to black, but this may create further problems if the registration is not perfect. This is often in evidence in mass-produced magazines and newspapers.

When white type is required to fulfill a particular design requirement, the most successful typefaces are those with strong serifs and a horizontal stress such as Souvenir, Congress and Bookman. These have the old style characteristics of little contrast between thick and thin strokes and strong serifs less likely to suffer from poor platemaking, registration or printing. Medium or semi-bold sans serifs can also be used but because of the stronger vertical stress of the sans serif form, increased line feed is desirable as a visual counter to that stress.

Limited use of coloured type can be effective if the typeface is sufficiently strong for good legibility and the quantity of body copy is limited. Obviously such thresholds can only be assessed by the designer in the context of the work in question.

Another common form of type misuse occurs with the combination of text over illustrative material. Black type over a plain colour can read quite well, but black text over a light but heavily textured background can become virtually indecipherable. This is a very common fault when type, particularly body copy, is combined with full colour photography.

For use in body copy, the three primary colours create similar problems as the straight white out of black style. The primary magenta, and the secondary red, green and violet colours are all tiring upon the eyes, whilst yellow on white is far too weak in tone for any degree of reasonable legibility. To a lesser degree, the same is true of cyan although because of its recessive characteristics it is not quite so tiring to read. Softer dark browns and greys can work well but should only really be used where a fifth colour and printing can be used specifically for the copy. This ensures a far cleaner, crisper image than could otherwise be achieved in general magazine production where any fifth colour has to be obtained by the four-colour process. The screening of fine type (below 15pt) is not good design; the edges lack clarity and again if the registration is fractionally out, legibility suffers further.

For use in body copy, the three primary colours create similar problems as the straight white out of black style. The primary magenta, and the secondary red, green and violet colours are all tiring upon the eyes, whilst yellow on white is far too weak in tone for any degree of reasonable legibility. To a lesser degree, the same is true of cyan although because of its recessive characteristics it is not quite so tiring to read. Softer dark browns and greys can work well but should only really be used where a fifth colour and printing can be used specifically for the copy. This ensures a far cleaner, crisper image than could otherwise be achieved in general magazine production where any fifth colour has to be obtained by the four-colour process. The screening of fine type (below 15pt) is not good design; the edges lack clarity and again if the registration is fractionally out, legibility suffers further.

For use in body copy, the three primary colours create similar problems as the straight white out of black style. The primary magenta, and the secondary red, green and violet colours are all tiring upon the eyes, whilst yellow on white is far too weak in tone for any degree of reasonable legibility. To a lesser degree, the same is true of cyan although because of its recessive characteristics it is not quite so tiring to read. Softer dark browns and greys can work well but should only really be used where a fifth colour and printing can be used specifically for the copy. This ensures a far cleaner, crisper image than could otherwise be achieved in general magazine production where any fifth colour has to be obtained by the four-colour process. The screening of fine type (below 15pt) is not good design; the edges lack clarity and again if the registration is fractionally out, legibility suffers further.

Typographic distortion

The almost unlimited possibilities created by computer typesetting can allow the inexperienced designer almost too much freedom. Many of these problems stem from the introduction of desktop publishing, and its use by inexperienced and untrained personnel.

Because it is possible to condense, expand, backslant and italicize type to any degree, typefaces can be over-distorted very easily. To maintain good readability type designers produce an internal balance within each character which contrasts vertical and horizontal stress. This is most noticeable within the Modern serif but it is also evident within a uniformly even sans serif typeface such as Helvetica or Univers. A closer study shows that there is a subtle variation between the vertical and horizontal and it is this that provides the fundamental optical balance of weight distribution.

When the computer condenses a face it only condenses its vertical stress. Thus the vertical strokes reduce in thickness whilst the horizontal weights remain constant. The operative should change the type font when a more condensed face is required, not destroy the existing image. The reasons for this are twofold: first, due to ignorance and second, a typesetting manufacturing management that is not prepared to invest properly in a well-balanced selection of typefaces.

Expansion of type causes similar distortion but it does not destroy the fundamental balance of the design as condensing does, since the relation between thick and thin becomes greater as the main vertical stress expands. Electronic modification of type has its place.

When copy is tight most people cannot spot an overall 2 per cent condensation. However, with every face there is a point where the design starts to deteriorate and it is at that point where the skill of the experienced typographer is required, who should know when to stop. Some faces can be reduced more than others. In general the greater the difference between the vertical and horizontal stresses to begin with, the greater the modification possible for condensing, or the less the difference between the stresses the greater the possibilities for expansion. However, modification of a letter like S, because of the weight and angle of the stem, will always be unsatisfactory.

Italicization created by distortion may work in some particular typefaces, but in some the results are unacceptable. The typeface may look reasonable but actually the design is not a genuine italic. Quite often the design of some characters; a, f, g, k and y in particular, will change quite considerably in the italic form. The serif will either be redrawn or perhaps omitted altogether. There is no way that a face can be truly italicized electronically, although it might in some instances produce a new acceptable typeface based upon the original.

Even when adopting the premise, 'If it looks right it is right' it still takes years of experience and judgement to know when a modification is right. That kind of experience cannot come overnight from operating a DTP keyboard as though it were a typewriter. Designers must always control technology and never allow technology to control them.

ABOVE: Whilst the above example contains a decorative quality, the natural stress of the letterform has been turned upside down. Although even weight is maintained within the vertical and horizontal strokes, the diagonal strokes (in the W, M and S) are totally out of sympathy with the rest of the type. This is because the basic typesetter or desk top programme cannot distort in proportion, it can only stretch or expand the horizontal leaving the vertical constant.

RIGHT: Expansion is far more satisfactory than condensation although it is not perfect. It works better because it exaggerates the natural balance between thick and thin stress, unlike condensing which destroys the natural stress.

BOTTOM LEFT: The hand-drawn logo can give a feel of distortion without losing any of the qualities of the correct stress and balance.

BOTTOM RIGHT: A good example of extreme distortion. Whilst most of these characters are acceptable as a new typeface, the stress of the S is wrong. The central curve is too thick in relation to the vertical weight of the other characters and should have been redrawn by hand.

118

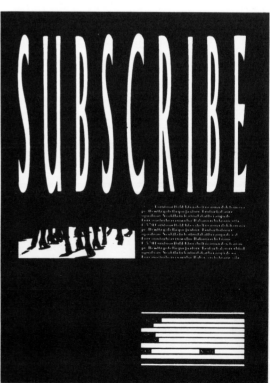

TYPOGRAPHY

TYPOGRAPHY

Y YYYYYYYYYYYYYYYYYYYYYYYYY Y

PPPPP P

OOOO O OOO

GGGGGGGGGGGG G GGG

RRRRRRRRRRRRRRRRRRRRRRRRRR

A A AAAAAAAAA AAAAA A

PPPPPPPPPP PPPPP

H HHHHHH

YYYYYYYYYYYYYYYYYY Y ?

?

Typographer meets computer! This image was produced by a graphic designer experimenting with a computerised typesetter. With the minimum of keystrokes letters have been condensed, expanded and repeated. The WYSIWIG (what-you-see-is-what-you-get) monitor enabled the designer to instantly see the results of each keystroke.

Bad type mixing

The possibilities of mixing different faces and the care that needs to be taken to obtain balance and compatability is by example and explanation. These typefaces have been deliberately altered from the original artwork in an attempt to produce examples of incompatability.

Lorem ipsum consectetur

Lorem ipsum dolor sit amet, consectetur adipiscing elit, sed diam zum nonnumy eiusmodn empor incidunt ut labore et dolore magna aliqua erar volupat. Ut enim adminim veniam, quis nostrud exercitation nisi ut aliquip ex ea commodo consequat. Duis autem vel eum irure dolor in reprehenderit in volupante velit esse moledtaie consequat, vel illum dolore eu. Lorem ipsum dolor sit amet, consectetur adipiscing elit, sed diam zum nonnumy eiusmodn empor incidunt ut labore et

Poor kerning

Poor kerning is unlikely to occur if the typesetter has equipment with automatic kerning programs. Without these the typesetter may have to hand kern the worst character combinations such as To, LT, y, r, etc. It may cost a little more but will help make a good job.

RAILWAYS

Descender/Ascender clash

Two or more lines used in a headline normally work better when the line feed is less than the type size. When implementing this style note the position of the ascenders and descenders, and ensure they do not clash.

Lorem ipsum
tetur adipisj
nonnumy e

1

Lorem ipsum consectetur

Lorem ipsum dolor sit amet, consectetur adipiscing elit, sed diam zum nonnumy eiusmodn empor incidunt ut labore et dolore magna aliqua erar volupat. Ut enim adminim veniam, quis nostrud exercitation nisi ut aliquip ex ea commodo consequat. Duis autem vel eum irure dolor in reprehenderit in volupante velit esse moledtaie consequat, vel illum dolore eu. Lorem ipsum dolor sit amet, consectetur adipiscing elit, sed diam zum nonnumy eiusmodn empor incidunt ut labore et dolore magna aliqua erar volupat. Ut enim

RAILWAYS

dolop sit ameq, consec-
ng elit, sed diam pum
shodn empor incidunt

Glossary

No glossary is exhaustive. This is restricted to terms a typographer is likely to encounter whilst dealing with typesetters, artists and designers. The current meaning of a word is generally given rather than any traditional terms as they were applied to hot metal typesetting.

A

A.A.
Abbreviation of 'author's alteration', used to identify any alteration in text or illustrative matter which is not a printer's error.

Accent Mark added to a letter in certain languages to indicate a change in pronunciation or stress etc.

Addendum Matter to be included in a book after the body copy has been set, which is printed separately at the beginning or end of the text.

Advertising rule Rule used to separate one magazine or press advertisement from another.

Align To arrange letters and words on the same horizontal or vertical line.

Alphabet length Horizontal measurement, in points or millimetres, of the length of the lowercase alphabet.

Alphanumeric Any system that combines letters and numbers.

Ampersand The symbol &; used as an abbreviation for the word 'and'.

Annotation Captions or numbers used on illustrative work.

Arabic numerals Numerals from 1 through to 9 and zero, as opposed to Roman numerals, I, II, III etc.

Arm Horizontal stroke in characters such as E, F and T that is free on one end.

Artwork All original copy, whether prepared by an artist, camera, or other mechanical means. Loosely speaking, any copy to be reproduced.

Ascender Top part of the lower case letters b, d, f, h, k, i, and t that rises above the x-height.

Asterisk *; usually used to indicate a footnote or give special emphasis.

Author's proof Proofs with 'literal' typographical errors corrected by the typesetter marked on them.

B

Backslant Typeface which slants backward, ie opposite to italic. The effect can be obtained by many headline machines and computer typesetters.

Bad break Incorrect end-of-line hyphenation, or a page beginning with either a widow or the end of hyphenated word.

Bad copy Any manuscript that is illegible, improperly edited, or otherwise unsatisfactory to the typesetter. Most typesetters charge extra to set from bad copy.

Banner Main headline across the full width of the page.

Bar Horizontal stroke in characters such as A, H, e, t.

Base line Imaginary line on which the base of the typeface (excluding descenders) rests.

Black letter Script with angular outlines developed in Germany which superceded the lighter roman of the 12th century. The term is also applied to types developed from it, such as Fraktur, Gothic and Old English.

Bleed Area of plate or print that extends (bleeds off) beyond the edge of the trimmed sheet. Applies mostly to photographs and areas of colour.

Blue line Blue line printed or drawn by the artist on artwork as a layout guide for the position of typesetting or artwork etc. Because the lines are a special blue they are not picked up when photographed for plate-making.

Body copy Also called body matter. Regular reading matter, or text, as opposed to display matter, headlines, etc.

Body size Overall depth of a piece of type measured in points.

Body type Also called text type, normally sizes between 6pt and 14pt, generally used for text matter.

Bold face Type with thickened strokes, normally a bolder version of the standard weight of type.

Book face Weight of typeface suitable for setting large areas of text.

Border Continuous decorative design arranged around text or illustration.

Box Item ruled off on all four sides usually with heavy rule or border.

Brackets *See* parentheses.

Break for colour To indicate or separate the parts of a mechanical for colour printing.

Break in copy Term indicating that part of the copy is missing.

Built fraction Fraction that is made up from two or more characters. For example, ⅞ would be made from a 7 followed by a / followed by an 8, as opposed to a piece fraction.

Bullet Solid circular, oval or square symbol used as ornamental or organizational device.

C

Calligraphy From the Greek, meaning beautiful handwriting. A calligrapher is a person who writes in an elegant traditional style.

Cap Abbreviation for capital letter.

Cap height Height of a capital letter from its baseline to top of character.

Capital letters, capitals Name of the upper case letters. It derives from the inscriptional letters at the head, or capital, of Roman columns.

Cap line Imaginary line that runs along the top of the capital letters.

Caps and smalls Typeset with most or all initials in capitals and other letters in small caps instead of lower case.

Caption Strictly speaking, the caption is the descriptive matter printed as a headline above an illustration. Usually refers to descriptive matter printed underneath an illustration.

Caret The symbol λ: Used in proof correction to indicate an insertion. The symbol was first used by scribes in the early century.

Carolingian script A 9th-century script developed for the Emperor Charlemagne's revision of grammars, bibles, church books etc.

Carry forward Instruction to transfer text to the next column or page.

Cast-off Calculation of how much space a given amount of copy will take in a given type size and measure.

Cathode ray tube (CRT) Electronic tube used, in one form of computer typesetting, to transmit letter images in the form of dots or lines onto photo-sensitive materials.

Centred Type placed in the centre of a measure.

Centre dot The centre dot can be of any size and is usually centred on the lowercase 'x-height' of the typeface with which it appears. When used with caps it should be centred between the cap-height.

Centre spread Centre two pages of a brochure, magazine, or a newspaper.

Central processing unit (CPU) Section of the computer containing the microchip which controls the interpretation and execution of instructions.

Character Any single unit of type font, whether it be a letter, numeral or punctuation mark (or space when calculating a character count).

Character count Calculation of the number of characters in a piece of copy.

Character generation Projection, or formation of typographic images onto the face of the cathode ray tube in CRT typesetting.

Cicero Continental equivalent of the pica, but fractionally larger. Used as a unit for measuring the width or measure of a line of type and the depth of a page. One Cicero = 4.511mm or 12 Didot points.

Clean proof Typesetter's proof free from errors.

Close spacing Type set with very little space between words.

Close up Instruction meaning to delete a space, to bring characters together.

Colophon Inscription formerly placed at the end of a book giving the title, printer's name, place and date of printing. In modern times it also refers, incorrectly, to a publisher's decorative device; the British equivalent of the American dingbat.

Column mm Measurement based on a space one column width and one mm deep. Often used when selling advertising space.

Column rule Fine rule used to separate columns.

Combination line and tone Combined block used to reproduce halftone photographs or illustrations with superimposed line letters, figures, diagrams etc.

Comp See comprehensive.

Compose To set copy in type. This is done by the compositor.

Compositor Also called the typesetter. The operator of the typesetting equipment.

Comprehensive Often referred to as a comp. An accurate layout showing type and illustrations in position, suitable as a finished presentation.

Computer typesetter Computer-controlled method of setting type. There are three basic kinds: photographic, CRT and laser generated.

Condensed face Typeface of elongated or narrow appearance.

Contact print Photographic print made by direct contact as opposed to enlargement or reduction.

Continuous-tone copy Image with a complete range of tones from black to white, for example photographs and painting.

Copy Raw material to be set in type by the typesetter.

Copyfitting The process of determining the area required for a given amount of copy in a specified typeface.

Counter Inside area of type such as the inside of the letter 'O'.

Crop To mark a part of a photograph or illustration in order that it either fits a given area or makes a better picture.

CRT See Cathode Ray Tube.

Cursive Typefaces that resemble handwriting, but without connected letters.

D

DTP See Desktop Publishing.

Dagger †; Footnote reference mark.

Dash –; A punctuation mark, usually known as an en or em rule.

Deadline Time beyond which copy/artwork is needed by people in the next stage of work.

Definition Degree of sharpness in a negative or print.

Delete Instruction to take out. The proof reader's mark looks like this:

Descender Lower part of letters such as g, j, p, q, y, and sometimes J and f that fall below the baseline.

Desktop publishing Computer software program which allows text to be arranged in a variety of styles and combined with illustrations and other graphics. Usually outputted to a laser printer held in-house, allowing production of near-artwork quality material.

Detail/layout paper Thin translucent paper with a hard surface used for layout and sketches.

Didot point Continental unit of measurement for type established by the French typefounder, Firmin Didot, in 1775. One didot point = 0.0148ins, 0.37592mm; one Anglo/American point equal 0.013838ins, 0.35mm

Digital typesetting Typesetting where the characters are broken down into a pattern of dots to form the actual character.

Dingbat A decorative device usually incorporated within a pi font.

Dipthong Pair of vowels pronounced as one, as in Cæsar.

Discretionary hyphen Hyphen which is keyboarded with the copy, which may or may not be used in the printed matter.

Display Printed matter to which prominence is given by its size and position. This includes prelims, part and chapter titles, headings, advertisements.

Display type Large typefaces designed for headings, etc. In general, sizes above 14pt are regarded as display sizes.

Dot leaders Series of dots that link items, used to guide the eye.

Double column Two columns side by side.

Double page spread Two facing pages which are treated as one in terms of design.

Dropped letter/initial Initial letter covering more than one line of type.

Dry-transfer lettering Form of lettering transferred to the page by burnishing each letter off the back of a sheet.

Dummy Prototype of a proposed book, brochure or leaflet in the correct style, weight and size.

E

Editing Reading copy for fact, spelling, grammar, and consistency of style.

Elite Smallest size of typewriter: 12 characters per inch as compared to the pica typewriter which has 10.

Ellipses Three dots (. . .) often used when omitting copy from quoted matter or to lead the eye to further copy.

Em Unit of linear measurement. The square of the type size being set. Its main function is in the specification of indentation for paragraphs. The 12pt em is known as the pica em, and is used to specify the measure of type.

Em dash Long dash the width of an em quad.

Em leader Horizontal series of dots or dashes evenly spaced one em from centre to centre.

En Measurement half the width of an em.

En-dash Dash the width of an en.

Even smalls Small caps used without full size capitals.

Exception dictionary Portion of the computer's memory in which exceptional words are stored.

F

Face Group or family to which any particular type design belongs.

Factor number Copyfitting number given to each composition size and typeface developed by the Monotype Corporation. The factor number expresses an average size of character.

Family Group of typefaces in a series with common characteristics in design, but of different weights such as italic, bold, condensed, expanded, etc.

Fat face Typeface with extensive contrast between the thin and thick strokes.

Film advance Distance by which the film/paper in the photo unit of the computer is advanced between lines. See line feed.

Filmsetting Process of using photographic means (on film or paper) to produce typesetting. It has almost totally replaced metal setting.

Finished artwork See mechanical.

Fine rule Rule of hair line thickness.

First proof Proofs submitted for checking by proof readers, copy editors etc.

First revise Proof pulled after errors have been corrected in the first proof.

Flush left (or right) Type that lines vertically to the left (or right).

Flush paragraphs Paragraphs in which the first word is not indented but set flush with the vertical line of the text.

Folio Page number.

Font A corruption of FOUNT.

Foot Margin at the bottom of a page; also the bottom edge of a book.

Footnote Short explanatory notes, printed at the foot of the page or at the end of a book.

Foreword Introductory remarks to a work or an author and not written by the author.

Format General appearance or style of a book including size, shape, paper quality, type face and binding.

Fount The complete set of characters of a typeface including punctuation, accents, fractions, etc.

Full point Full stop/period.

G

Galley proof First proof from the typesetter used for checking printers errors and for checking size and position against the layout.

Grid Measuring guide used by designers to help ensure consistency. The grid shows type widths, picture areas, trim sizes and margins and is used particularly where the work has more than one page.

Grotesk / grotesque Anothr name for sans serif typefaces.

Gutter Channel running through the centre of a page, book or brochure.

H

H & J (Hyphenation and Justification) Ability of the computer to hyphenate and justify lines automatically. There are various methods available: discretionary, logic exception dictionary and true dictionary.

Hairline Thin strokes of a typeface.

Hairline rule Thinest of rules.

Half tone The process by which various shades of grey are simulated by black dots of various sizes in a pattern.

Hanging-indent Indented setting where the first line of each paragraph is set full-out to the column measure and the remaining lines are indented.

Hanging punctuation Punctuation which hangs outside the measure, so that the right hand side of the column aligns visually.

Headline Large type in an advertisement, brochure or leaflet that draws the reader's attention to the design.

Heading Bold or display type used to emphasise copy.

Headliner Machine able to produce display sizes of type. The operator has visual control over spacing, distortion and size.

Hot metal setting Mechanical typesetting that involves each character to be used cast in hot molten metal.

House corrections Alterations made to proofs or script by the publisher or printer, as distinct from those made by the author.

House style Style or spelling, punctuation, spacing and typographical layout used in a printing or publishing house to ensure consistent treatment of copy during typesetting.

Hung initial Display letter that is set outside the text in the left-hand margin.

Hyphenation & Justification See H & J.

I

Illustration General term for any form of drawing, diagram, halftone, or colour image included within the artwork of a piece of print.

Imposition Plan for, and the arrangement of, pages in press form so they will appear in the correct order when printed, folded, bound and trimmed.

Imprint Name of the printer, publisher, date and place of printing. Required by law if the paper or book is to be published.

Indent Positioning of type, usually the first line of paragraph, in from the edge of the left hand margin.

Inferior figures Small letters or figures usually printed on or below the baseline, for example in chemical formulae such as H_2O.

Initial First letter of a body of copy, which can be set in a larger size type for decoration or emphasis. Often used to begin a chapter of a book. *See also* drop, hung and raised initials.

Initial caps The setting of the first word or phrase of the copy in capitals.

Interline spacing Also called line feed, instead of the old hot metal term of leading.

Italic Letterforms that slope to the right. *Looks like this.*

J

Jacket Paper wrapper in which a book is sold.

Jobbing work Small everyday printing such as display cards, letterheadings, labels, handbills and other printing – as distinct from book or magazine work.

Justify Act of justifying lines of type to a specific measure, right and left, by equally spacing each word within each line to make it fit the full measure.

K

Kerning Adjustment of space between characters so that part of one extends over the body of the next. Modern typesetters include kerning programmes as standard for letter spacing. Kerned letters produce uniform letter spacing closing up excessive space encountered between such combinations as LY and Te. *See also* Letterfit.

Kerned letters Part of the letter which projects beyond the body or shank, thus overlapping an adjacent character. Kerned letters are common in italic, script, and swash fonts.

Keyline Outlines on artwork denoting the position of illustrative matter as a guide for the platemaker and printer.

Key size Alternative method of measuring type. Key size calculates the size of type by its cap height, unlike the traditional method which measures type by its overall depth. Ideal systems when mixing type on line as consistency of cap height is always maintained.

L

Large fractions Fractions made up of text-size numbers, as opposed to case fractions.

Layout Outline or sketch which gives the general appearance of the printed page, indicating the relationship between text and illustration.

Layout paper See detail paper.

L.C. (l.c.) Lower case characters of a font.

Leading Strips of metal or brass of varying thickness used to space out headings and text in the times of hot metal setting and letterpress printing. The term is still used as a means of expressing line feed.

Letterspacing Insertion of space between the letters of word to improve the appearance of a line of type. *See also* kerning.

Letterfit Quality of space between the individual characters. Letterfit should be uniform and allow for good legibility. Advanced kerning programmes on modern typesetters achieve first class 'letterfit' combinations.

Letterspace Space between letters.

Ligature Characters joined together such as fi, ff and ffi.

Light face Lighter version of the standard weight of typeface.

Line drawing Artwork consisting of solid black lines. A drawing without half tones.

Line feed Space between each line of type, formerly known as leading.

Line length See measure.

Line overlay Line work put on an overlay to pre-separate lines from halftones or show the position of different colours. Used in the preparation of artwork.

Line up When two lines of type, or a line of type and illustration, align to the same imaginary horizontal or vertical line.

Logotype Often referred to as a logo. Character(s) designed as a trademark or company signature.

Lower case Small letters in a font of type. Indicated as l.c.

M

Machine proof Final proof taken from the printing press. Machine proofs provide the final opportunity for the correction of mistakes.

Makeup Assembling the various typographic and artwork elements into a form ready for platemaking.

Manuscript Literally, a work written by hand. It refers either to a book written before the invention of printing or the typed work which an author submits for publication, in which case it is also known as a typescript.

Margins Blank edges on a printed page which surround the text and illustrative matter.

Marked proof The proof, usually in galleys, supplied

to the author for correction. It contains the corrections and queries made by the printer's reader.

Mark up The specification of every detail needed for the typesetter to set the copy.

Masthead Any design or logotype used as identification by a newspaper or publication.

Measure Width of a setting measured in pica ems or millimetres.

Mechanical An American term for artwork. Preparation of copy to make it camera-ready with all type design elements pasted in position. Also contains any necessary instructions regarding the laying of tints, halftones etc.

Metric system European system or decimal measurement. The basic unit for designers is the millimetre (mm) and occasionally the centimetre (cm).

Minus letterspacing Reduction of the normal space allocated between characters.

Minus linespacing When line feed (the measurement from base line to base line) is less than the body size of the typeface. Should only be used when ascenders and descenders do not touch, unless a special effect is required.

Misprint A typographical error.

Modern face Term used to describe the type style developed in the late 18th century. A typeface with vertical stress, strong contrast and unbracketed fine serifs.

O

Old style The type style based on 16th-century letterforms, characterized

by diagonal stress and sloped, bracketed serifs.

Old style figures Also called hanging figures. Numerals that vary in size, some having ascenders and others descenders: 1234567890. As opposed to lining figures.

Open matter Type set with abundant line spacing or containing many short lines.

Ornaments Type ornaments used to embellish page borders, chapter headings, title pages etc.

Orphan Last word or a paragraph (or line) that stands at the top of the following column or page by itself.

Outline letters Open characters made from solid ones by putting a line on the outside edge of a letter.

P

Pamphlet Booklet of a few pages.

Page proofs Preliminary print for checking against original manuscript and artwork for correct colour and positioning of tints, photographs, etc.

Pagination The numbering of the pages in a book.

Paragraph mark Typographical elements used to direct the eye to the beginning of a paragraph (¶). Often used when the paragraph is not intended.

Parenthesis ( ): punctuation mark or ornament. They are usually called brackets.

Paste-up Positioning of artwork ready for production. *See also* mechanical.

PE Abbreviation for 'Printer's error' as opposed to AA.

Period Punctuation mark, the full stop.

Phototypesetting Also known as Photocomposition. The production of manuscript by projecting type images onto photographic film or paper.

Pica (em) Typographical measurement equal to 12pts (approximately 1/6th of an inch or 4.25mm).

Pi characters Special characters not usually included in a type font, such as special ligatures, accented letters, mathematical signs and reference signs. E.g. Φ e μ ϱ ω.

Piece fraction These come in three styles. Adaptable, made up of three separate characters; two text size numerals separated by a slash (3/4). Case fractions, which are small-numbered fractions available as a single character (⅜). Piece fractions, which are small-numbered fractions made up of three or more elements: nominator, slash or separating rule, and the denominator.

Point Standard unit of typograhic measurement. The British/American point is equal to 0.01383in, approx 0.35mm (approximately 1/72 of an inch).

Portrait Upright image or page.

Primary letters Lower case letters without ascenders or descenders, such as a, c, e, m, n etc.

Print run Number of copies to be printed.

Proof Impression obtained from an inked plate, stone screen, block or type in order to check the progress and accuracy of the work. Also called a pull.

Proofreader Person who reads the type that has been set against the

marked-up typescript, checking for corrections of style, spelling, punctuation, etc.

Proofreaders marks Marks made by the proofreader to indicate alterations and corrections that are required to the proof. Symbols are standard throughout the industry.

Q

Quad (verb) To space out the blank portion of a line to its full measure. A hot metal term that is now more commonly referred to as 'flush left' 'flush right' and 'centred'. *See* unjustified type.

R

Ragged *See* unjustified type.

Raised initial Display letter that base-aligns with the first line of text.

Range Instruction to align the right or left-hand edge of a block vertically to the type above or below it. *See* also unjustified type.

Reader *See* proofreader.

Reference mark Symbol used to direct the reader from the text to a footnote or other reference. The more common marks are as follows:
* Star or asterisk
 § Section   † Dagger
|| Parallels   ¶ Paragraph.
†† Double dagger

Register The correct alignment of pages with the margins in order. Also the correct positioning of one colour upon another in colour printing.

Register marks The crosses, triangles and other devices used in colour printing to position the paper correctly.

Reproduction proofs Also called repro. High quality proofs on art paper, which can be used as art work.

Rivers Streaks of white spacing in text produced when spaces in consecutive lines of type coincide.

Revise Change in instruction that alters copy in any stage prior to final artwork.

Roman Name often applied to the Latin alphabet as it is used in English and European languages. Also used to identify upright type as distinct from italic.

Roman numerals Roman letters in current use as numerals until the tenth century AD I, II, III, IV, etc.

Rough Sketch giving a general idea of the size and position of the various elements of the design.

Rule Line used for a variety of design effects including borders, separating lines and boxes. Rules can also be dotted, dashed or decorative.

Run round Text type fitting closely around an irregular shape.

Run on Instruction for text to continue without a new paragraph. A run-on chapter is one which does not begin on a new page.

S

Sans serif Typeface without serifs, usually without stroke contrast.

Script Typeface designed to imitate handwriting.

Serif Small terminal stroke at the end of the main stroke of a letter.

Set close Instruction to set type with the minimum of space between the individual characters and words.

Set solid Instruction to set type without extra line feed (leading).

Set width Also called set size, or set. The width of each individual character within a font. This space, measured in units, can be increased or decreased to adjust the letter spacing.

Slab serif *See* square serif.

Small capitals Capital letters which are smaller than the standard and unusually aligned with the x height of the type face.

Solid Type set with minimal line feed.

Spec (specification) To calculate and order typographical setting.

Square serif Typeface in which the serifs are of a similar weight to the main stem as in the Rockwell, Lubalin and Egyptian typefaces.

S.S. Abbreviation for same size. Also indicated S/S.

Stem Straight vertical stroke, or main straight diagonal stroke in a letter which has no vertical strokes.

Stet Latin word meaning 'let it stand' written in the margin in proof corrections to cancel a previously marked correction.

Stress Direction of thickening in a curved stroke.

Sub-heading Heading for a division of a chapter or section.

Sub-title Phrase, often explanatory, which follows a title of a book.

Superior letters or figures *See* superscript.

Superscript Small symbol, numeral or letter that prints above the x-height and to the side of another character as in this example[4]. Also called superior letter or figure, particularly when used to refer to a citation source.

Swash letters Old face italic types with calligraphic flourishes.

T

Tabular matter Type set in rows and columns under titles.

Text Body copy of a page or book, as opposed to headings.

Text type Main body type, usually smaller in size than 14pt.

Thumbnails Small, rough sketches.

Tint Photomechanical reduction in strength of a solid colour by screening.

Title page Right hand page at the front of a book which bears the title, the names of the author and publisher, the place of publication and other relevant information.

Titling Headline type which is only available in capitals.

Transfer type *See* dry-transfer lettering.

Transitional Type forms invented in the mid eighteenth century bridging the Old Face and Modern styles. They include Fournier and Baskerville.

Transpose To change the order of the letters, words, lines or paragraphs.

Transposition Typographic error in which the letters are incorrectly placed, ie tihs instead of this.

Trim size Final size of a printed work after trimming. When preparing artwork allowance must always be made for trim.

Type Letters of the alphabet and all the other characters used singly or collectively.

Type area Area on the page designated to contain text and illustrative matter.

Type family Range of typeface designs that are variations of one basic style of design. Thus we have

Helvetica **bold**, light, *italic*, condensed etc.

Type mark-up *See* mark-up.

Typescript Typed manuscript.

Typesetter Person who sets type, or a shortening of computer typesetter.

Typesetting Copy produced by the computer typesetter.

Type size There are two different methods of defining type size, one: by the height or the capital letter (see key size) and two: by the type faces overall depth measured from the top of the highest character to the bottom of the lowest.

Type style Variation within a typeface: **medium, bold,** *italic*, condensed etc.

Typographer Person who designs the typographical layout of a proposed printed work. Also the designer of typefaces.

U

U & l.c. Abbreviation of upper and lower case.

Uncial Hand-drawn book face used by the Romans and early Christians, typified by the heavy, squat form of the rounded O.

Underscore A rule directly below a line of type.

Upper case Capital letters of a typeface.

Unit Variable measurement based on the division of the em or set size into equal increments.

Unitization Designing the font charactrs to width groups. The width groups are measured in units and are the basis for the counting mechanism of the computer typesetting equipment. Width units can be based on the em or the set size of the font.

Unit system Counting method first developed by

Monotype and now used by some typewriters and all computer typesetting systems to measure, in units, the width of the individual characters and spaces being set. By counting the total accumulated units the computer can determine the inter-word spacing when the line is ready to be justified, and determine how much space is left for justification.

Unit value Fixed unit width of individual characters.

Unjustified type Lines of type set to different lengths aligning to the left, right or centre.

Uppercase Capital letters of a typeface ie A B C etc.

V

Visual *See* layout.

W

Weight Degree of boldness of a typeface. Most typefaces are designed in light, **medium** and **bold**. These are known as the different weights.

Widow Single word or part of a hyphenated word at the end of a paragraph left on a line of its own.

Word break Device of hyphenating a word between syllables so it can be split into two sections to regulate line length in a text.

Word spacing Adding or reducing space between words to complete justification.

Wrong font Indication that a letter of the wrong size or font has been set by mistake. It is abbreviated as w.f.

X

X-height Height of the lowercase letters without either ascender or descender.

Index

Picture Credits

Apple Business Magazine/ Robert Clifford: pages 105 and 106.

Bauhaus Archiv: pages 98 and 99.

Neville Brody: pages 110 (third right) and 111 (top left). Neville Brody Catalogue: page 118. Neville Brody/*Arena*: page 111 (top left & bottom right). Neville Brody/*City Limits*: page 111 (middle right). Neville Brody/*Comag*: page 111 (middle left). Neville Brody/*The Face*: pages 110 (right & bottom) and 111 (top right). Neville Brody/*Post*: page 110 (top left).

CBS Records: page 17 (top & middle).

ET Archive: pages 33, 34, 35, 40, 45 (middle) and 59.

Ford: page 22 (middle right).

Michael Freeman: 10, 11, 12, 13 and 32.

Terry Jeavons: page 119.

Lacerba: pages 41, 78 and 79.

Herb Lubalin Study Centre of Design and Typography: pages 20, 21 and 59 (bottom).

The Mansell Collection: page 44 (top left).

The Monotype Corporation: page 44 (top right & bottom right).

Peter Newark: page 45 (top, bottom left & right).

Robert Opie: pages 18 and 19.

Pentagram Design Ltd: pages 16, 17 (bottom), 22 (top & bottom left), 23, 24, 25, 26, 66/67 and 72/73.

Plessey: page 22 (middle left).

David Quay: pages 14 and 15.

Guy Ryecart: page 87.

St Bride's Printing Library: pages 28, 29, 36, 37, 38, 39 (middle) and 63.

The Times: page 39 (top).